LET'S STUDY
THE LETTERS
OF JOHN

1 Cor 7 v6 / 8&v8 ~~v12~~ 1 Cor 7 v12

2 Cor 1 Cor 1 Cor 7 v4⊕ must have the word

1 Cor

2 Cor 8 v8

tradition is the living faith of the Dead

Traditionalism is the dead faith of the living

0131 441 7079

2222222

D Alison Nicholls
Nicholson
Nicholls.

MOD - MacLeod -

Ian Hamilton books =

God knows hea

PRATT   Dog!

(Emcrdv 30 - apple)

In the same series:

LET'S STUDY MARK by Sinclair B. Ferguson
LET'S STUDY MATTHEW by Mark E. Ross
LET'S STUDY LUKE by Douglas J. W. Milne
LET'S STUDY JOHN by Mark G. Johnston
LET'S STUDY ACTS by Dennis E. Johnson
LET'S STUDY 1 CORINTHIANS by David Jackman
LET'S STUDY 2 CORINTHIANS by Derek Prime
LET'S STUDY GALATIANS by Derek Thomas
LET'S STUDY EPHESIANS by Sinclair B. Ferguson
LET'S STUDY PHILIPPIANS by Sinclair B. Ferguson
LET'S STUDY 1 & 2 THESSALONIANS by Andrew W. Young
LET'S STUDY HEBREWS by Hywel R. Jones
LET'S STUDY 1 PETER by William W. Harrell
LET'S STUDY 2 PETER & JUDE by Mark G. Johnston
LET'S STUDY REVELATION by Derek Thomas

Series Editor: SINCLAIR B. FERGUSON

Let's Study

THE LETTERS
OF JOHN

Ian Hamilton

THE BANNER OF TRUTH TRUST

THE BANNER OF TRUTH TRUST
3 Murrayfield Road, Edinburgh EH12 6EL, UK
P.O. Box 621, Carlisle, PA 17013, USA

*

© Ian Hamilton 2008
ISBN: 978 1 84871 013 9

*

Typeset in 11/12.5 pt Ehrhardt MT at the
Banner of Truth Trust, Edinburgh

Printed in the U.S.A. by
Versa Press, Inc.,
East Peoria, IL

TO JOAN,
THE BEST OF WIVES
AND DAVID, JONATHAN,
REBECCA, AND SARAH,
THE BEST OF CHILDREN

Contents

Publisher's Preface

*L*et's Study the Letters of John is part of a series of books which explain and apply the message of Scripture. The series is designed to meet a specific and important need in the church. While not technical commentaries, the volumes comment on the text of a biblical book; and, without being merely lists of practical applications, they are concerned with the ways in which the teaching of Scripture can affect and transform our lives today. Understanding the Bible's message and applying its teaching are the aims.

Like other volumes in the series, *Let's Study the Letters of John* seeks to combine explanation and application. Its concern is to be helpful to ordinary Christian people by encouraging them to understand the message of the Bible and apply it to their own lives. The reader in view is not the person who is interested in all the detailed questions which fascinate the scholar, although behind the writing of each study lies an appreciation for careful and detailed scholarship. The aim is exposition of Scripture written in the language of a friend, seated alongside you with an open Bible.

Let's Study the Letters of John is designed to be used in various contexts. It can be used simply as an aid for individual Bible study. Some may find it helpful to use in their devotions with husband or wife, or to read in the context of the whole family.

In order to make these studies more useful, not only for individual use but also for group study in Sunday School classes and home, church, or college, study guide material will be found on pp. 119. Sometimes we come away frustrated rather than helped by group discussions. Frequently that is because we have been encouraged to discuss a passage of Scripture which we do not understand very well in the first place. Understanding must always be the foundation for enriching discussion and for thoughtful, practical application. Thus, in addition to the exposition of the letters, the additional material provides questions to encourage personal thought and study, or to be used as discussion starters. The Group Study Guide divides the material into thirteen sections and provides direction for leading and participating in group study and discussion.

Introduction to 1 John

Most of the Letters in the New Testament were written in response to problems or difficulties being experienced in congregations. Their purpose was to teach, reprove, correct and train God's people in righteousness and equip them for every good work (see *2 Tim.* 3:16–17). This is certainly the purpose of John's first letter.

We are given no indication as to who the recipients of this letter were, or where they came from. Clearly John knows them. He calls them his 'little children' (2:1, 12, 28) and his 'beloved' (2:7; 4:1, 7). The letter shows us that they were being deeply unsettled in their faith. 'Antichrists' (2:18), 'false prophets' (4:1), had come among them and were denying fundamental Christian truths. They were rejecting the truth that Jesus truly had 'come in the flesh' (4:2), that he was 'the Christ' (2:22). They professed to know God and have fellowship with him, but they continued to 'walk in darkness' (1:6), they did not 'keep his commandments' (2:4) and they were narrow-hearted towards Christians in need (3:14–15, 17–18).

The profoundly tragic thing was that these 'antichrists' had once been part of Christ's church (2:19). Jesus himself had warned his disciples: 'Beware of false prophets, who come to you in sheep's clothing but inwardly are ravenous wolves' (*Matt.* 7:15). Similarly Paul warned the Ephesian elders that after his departure 'fierce wolves will come in among you, not sparing the flock' (*Acts* 20:29).

John's concern for the spiritual good of his 'little children' prompted him to write this letter. 1 John is polemical, but it is above all deeply pastoral. John never loses sight of the false teachers who were unsettling the faith of his 'beloved children', and he continually seeks to expose their antichristian teachings. His main concern, however, is to encourage and reassure his readers (see, for example, 5:13).

The 'antichrists' continued to claim that they were Christians, God's children, although they had separated themselves from God's people (2:19). As we noted already, they claimed that they had fellowship with God, even though they walked 'in darkness' (1:6). They claimed to know God, but did not keep his commandments (2:4). Throughout his Letter, John seeks to expose the falseness of their claims and show what a dangerous spiritual state they were in. More than anything, he wants to reassure his 'little children' that they truly are God's children and that these separatists are antichristian impostors.

The strong language John uses to describe the men who were denying the fundamentals of the gospel and unsettling the faith of God's people ('antichrists', 'false prophets', 'deceivers') is not, then, an expression of a nasty intolerance. This is what these men *were* (compare this with Jesus' description of the Pharisaic false teachers in his day, *Matt.* 23:13, 16, 25, 27–28, 33).

John is therefore writing as a deeply concerned pastor and his 'holy invective' is an expression of his opposition to men who were dishonouring the Saviour, disturbing his church and hiding the saving gospel of God's grace from a perishing world. For John, heresy was more to be feared than martyrdom. Right belief is not a theological nicety, it is necessary for salvation. Unbelief is the ultimate horror because it leaves the sinner under God's wrath (see *John* 3:36). John is responding, then, as a loving pastor to poisonous teaching and ungodly teachers.

The warning notes sounded throughout John's three Letters need to be heeded in our day. We live in an age of doctrinal indifference. Truth is often the first casualty in the desire for church unity, an imagined stumbling-block to Christians sharing the gospel with the world. But what is the gospel if it is not the revelation of God's truth and grace in his Son Jesus Christ? Paul was not being narrow-minded or blindly intolerant when he wrote to the Galatians, 'Even if we or an angel from heaven should preach to you a gospel contrary to the one we preached to you, let him be accursed' (*Gal.* 1:8). On the contrary, he wrote as a man who knew that God's truth was not negotiable. It was his concern for Christ's honour, the eternal safety of sinners, and the purity of Christ's church that compelled him to write as he did.

The main purpose of 1 John is clearly stated: 'I write these things to you who believe in the name of the Son of God that you may know that you have eternal life' (5:13). Just as John wrote his Gospel to win people to faith in Christ (*John* 20:31), so he now wrote to reassure his 'little children' who had come to faith. He does this in a way that would both encourage true believers and expose false teachers, by highlighting a number of 'tests' designed to distinguish the genuine from the counterfeit: a *doctrinal* test (see 2:22–23; 5:5, 10); a *moral* test (see 1:5–7; 2:4–6); and a *social* test (3:14, 17–18, 4:8).

The New Testament is very aware of the danger of counterfeit Christians (see *2 Cor.* 13:5) and John wants his 'little children' to be sure they are the Lord's, and to know how to recognize counterfeit believers. We can be sure that the tests John highlighted in writing to his first-century readers are as relevant to us living in the early years of the twenty-first century. God's Word tells us that infiltrating impostors will afflict the church throughout its history (see *2 Tim.* 3:1–13). Therefore we must 'watch and pray', 'follow the pattern of sound words' (*2 Tim.* 1:13), and 'contend for the faith that was once for all delivered to the saints' (*Jude* 3).

AUTHORSHIP

Thus far we have assumed that 'John' was the apostle John, who also wrote the Gospel that bears his name. However, the Letter (like the Letter to the Hebrews) nowhere tells us who the author is. There are, all the same, good reasons why the Letter is entitled in our Bibles, 'The First Letter of John'. Three in particular stand out.

First, the church in its earliest days was unanimous in ascribing this Letter (and 2 and 3 *John*) to John the apostle. Whenever the early church Fathers quote from this Letter, they ascribe its authorship to John. There was never a dispute over who the author was.

Second, the language, ideas and patterns of thought in this Letter remarkably echo what we read in the Gospel of John (John is certainly the author of the Gospel that bears his name, see *John* 21:24). Words and themes such as 'life', 'eternal life', 'darkness', 'fellowship', 'love', 'truth', and 'obedience' are common to John's Gospel and John's Letters. In John's Gospel and in this first Letter we read of the conflict between light and darkness (*John* 3:19–21 and *1 John* 1:5–6); of the God who is light and love (*John* 1:4–9; 3:16 and *1 John* 1:5; 4:8, 10); of the absolute necessity of loving one another (*John* 13:34–35 and *1 John* 3:11–18; 4:8,21; 5:2); of Christ, and those who believe in him, overcoming the world (*John* 16:33 and *1 John* 5:4); of Christ being the truth (*John* 1:14, 17; 14:6 and *1 John* 5:20).

Third, in 1:1–4 the writer repeatedly emphasizes the eyewitness nature of the testimony contained in the letter. *1 John* 1:1 in particular, places special emphasis on what the writer himself has heard, seen, looked upon, and touched. It is sometimes pointed out that the use of the first-person plural in the introduction does not conclusively prove the author to be an eyewitness participant in the events he writes about, since first-person plurals occur later in the letter with reference to the common experience of all Christians (for example, 4:13). But if all the writer is doing in his introduction is alluding to general Christian experience (that is, knowledge of the incarnation) it is hard to see how this could serve as any authentication of his message, which clearly seems to be the point of the opening verses. It appears, rather, that the author intends by his statements in verses 1–3 to indicate that he was one of the original eyewitnesses of the life and ministry of Jesus on earth, and that he intends to associate himself with the other original eyewitnesses, Christ's own apostles.

OCCASION

John has heard news that has deeply disturbed him and he writes to minister the pastoral help God's people were greatly in need of. There is no indication from within *1 John* of the particular church or group of churches he is writing to. It has long been held, however, that *1 John* is a general letter, written by him to congregations in Asia Minor, modern-day Turkey.

Throughout the Letter, John writes with warmth, seriousness and urgency.

1 JOHN

I

The Word of Life

That which was from the beginning, which we have heard, which we have seen with our eyes, which we looked upon and have touched with our hands, concerning the word of life— ² the life was made manifest, and we have seen it, and testify to it and proclaim to you the eternal life, which was with the Father and was made manifest to us— ³ that which we have seen and heard we proclaim also to you, so that you too may have fellowship with us; and indeed our fellowship is with the Father and with his Son Jesus Christ. ⁴ And we are writing these things so that our joy may be complete (1 John 1:1–4).

John, perhaps surprisingly, launches into his letter without any greeting or personal reference, as does the Letter to the Hebrews. Perhaps the urgency of the situation (insidious and spreading heresy) compelled him to forego the normal literary conventions. In these opening verses he tells us three vital things about the gospel:

First, *he affirms the historical fact and reliability of the gospel.* The verbs John uses are all calculated to make one great point: the gospel of our Lord Jesus Christ is not a speculation, or an ideal, or an opinion; it is a fact.

> *That which was from the beginning, which we have heard, which we have seen with our eyes, which we looked upon and have touched with our hands . . . was made manifest . . .*

[1]

It has been suggested that John is talking about the message of Christ rather than the person of Christ in these opening verses. Certainly in verse 5, John writes, 'This is the message we have heard . . .'. However, it is more likely that John is writing about Christ himself. While he does use a succession of neuter pronouns: 'That which . . . which . . . which . . .', what follows tells us that he is thinking about Christ himself: 'which we have seen with our eyes, which we have looked upon and have touched with our hands . . . the life was made manifest and we have seen it'. John is actually inviting us to see that the message of Christ and the person of Christ are one; indeed, Jesus Christ *is* the gospel.

We must not miss the echo of *John* chapter 1: he was 'with the Father', but was 'made manifest to us' (verse 2). The incarnation of the Son of God lies at the very heart of the Christian faith. In no other way could God deal justly with the sin that set us under his just judgment and provide us with the righteousness that would fit us for fellowship with him, and ultimately for his presence. In the God-Man, God was reconciling the world to himself (*2 Cor.* 5:19). The Jesus of history is the Christ of faith.

Second, *John highlights the essential core and content of the gospel.* He describes Jesus as 'the word of life' (verse 1) and as 'the eternal life which was with the Father' (verse 2). Both of these echo statements in John's Gospel – see *John* 1:1–4; 17:3. Jesus is 'the word of life'; he is the self-revelation of God who is life. In Jesus, God has disclosed himself savingly. God's eternal Word, his own and only-begotten Son, became flesh. This is the heart of the good news.

This is the Jesus that the church proclaims to the world, and the world stumbles over. Probably nothing more infuriates our world than the Bible's insistence on the uniqueness of Christ; that he is the self-revelation of the eternal God and the only Giver of life. But, says John, this is an indisputable fact. In Jesus Christ we are brought face to face with the true and living God (see *John* 1:1–3, 14,18). The gospel of Jesus Christ is not one of a number of options for men and women to consider, it is the one and only way for sinners to be reconciled to God and rescued from the coming wrath. How could it be otherwise, when Jesus is who he is, 'the eternal life, which was with the Father'.

'Eternal life', then, is a person (see *John* 17:3). This truth helps explain why 'union with Christ' is so central in the New Testament's understanding of salvation. Unless and until we are united to Christ, who is 'the eternal life', we remain under God's wrath, facing the nightmare prospect of eternal death. Indeed, Paul's most common description of a believer is that he or she is 'in Christ'.

Third, *John declares the great purpose of the gospel:* 'so that you too may have fellowship with us'. 'Fellowship' is one of the New Testament's great words. It means to live a shared life. In classical Greek it was sometimes used to describe the marriage union, the most intimate and precious of human relationships.

Consider the order of John's words. Would we not have put 'with the Father' and 'with his Son' before 'with us'? John is highlighting, quite dramatically, the importance of belonging to the people who have 'fellowship with the Father and with his Son Jesus Christ'. God's purpose in rescuing sinners is not only to save them from hell, but to bring them into the fellowship of his family. This highlights one of our great needs today; to recover the importance of the church, the 'household of faith', the family of God. The great significance of belonging to the fellowship of God's people is that its 'fellowship is with the Father and with his Son Jesus Christ'.

In his book, *Communion with God*,[1] John Owen richly develops the multi-faceted communion or fellowship that believers enjoy with the three persons of the Trinity. The Triune God is indivisible; but his Persons are not indistinguishable. Owen notes that in the New Testament, the Father is most often viewed as the One who loved us and gave his Son for us; the Son as the One who in grace came and gave himself for us; and the Holy Spirit as the One who applies to our lives the blessings and comforts of the gospel. So, says Owen, we have fellowship with the Father in love, not exclusively but pre-eminently; we have fellowship with the Son in grace, both personal and purchased grace – not exclusively but pre-eminently; we have fellowship with the Spirit in the comfort he ministers to us – again, not exclusively but pre-eminently. If nothing else, what John writes here highlights the richness, wonder and unfathomableness of the church's communion with God.

[1] *The Works of John Owen*, vol. 2 (London: Banner of Truth, 1965), pp. 5–268.

The saved life is lived, then, in fellowship with God and with his people. The implications of this for Christian living are immense. Too often Christians are guilty of living, worshipping and serving with little reference to 'the family'. The church is often an appendage, not the context, of our lives.

What John writes here challenges the individualism that makes self the hub of the universe. God wants us to understand that we are saved to belong. Without this 'fellowship' our joy cannot be complete (verse 4b). He is writing not merely to protect his 'little children' from error and give them assurance of salvation. Here he is writing so that 'our [or possibly 'your'] joy may be complete'. John is probably looking beyond this world to the world to come, where, in God's nearer presence there will be 'fullness of joy' (*Psa.* 16:11). But that 'fullness of joy' is experienced in fellowship with all God's redeemed people.

All this underlines our need to be more aware than we possibly are that the church is 'the body of Christ', 'the temple of the Holy Spirit', 'the household of faith', the one 'bride of Christ'. Salvation not only brings us into Christ, it brings us into the body of Christ, his church.

2

Walking in the Light

*T*his is the message we have heard from him and proclaim to you,
that God is light, and in him is no darkness at all. *⁶ If we say
we have fellowship with him while we walk in darkness, we lie and
do not practise the truth. ⁷ But if we walk in the light, as he is in the
light, we have fellowship with one another, and the blood of Jesus his
Son cleanses us from all sin. ⁸ If we say we have no sin, we deceive
ourselves, and the truth is not in us. ⁹ If we confess our sins, he is faithful and just to forgive us our sins and to cleanse us from all unrighteousness. ¹⁰ If we say we have not sinned, we make him a liar, and his
word is not in us* (1 John 1:5–10).

Much of what John writes is shaped to counteract the teaching
of the 'false prophets' (4:1) who were unsettling his readers.
In these verses he highlights three claims made by them and exposes their deceit. Before he does so, he reminds us who God is. False
teaching is almost always the result of losing sight of, or of denying,
who God is. The message that *'God is light'* was heard from Jesus
himself: it was 'from him'. John is probably summarizing Jesus'
extensive teaching on God. This 'message' is not something that
John, or others, invented. Here, then, is one of the Bible's com-
prehensive statements about God. He is light, and 'in him is no
darkness at all'. One of the main thrusts of the false teaching John
is exposing was its claim that it did not really matter how one lived;
what mattered was that one knew God. But the God the gospel
brings us to know, is the God who is light, and in whom there is
no darkness at all.

What does John mean when he tells us, 'God is light, and in
him is no darkness at all'? It seems clear from the context that he

is highlighting God's moral purity. The three claims of the false teachers that follow all assume that God and sin can easily co-exist. John could not be more categorical: 'God is light, and in him is no darkness at all.' God and sin, in all its forms, are mutually exclusive (*Hab.* 1:13). This is the uniform teaching of the whole Bible (consider *Isa.* 6:1–5; *Rev.* 21:27). In the theological and moral confusion that reigns throughout the church today, we need to make every effort to 'Strive . . . for the holiness without which no-one will see the Lord' (*Heb.*12:14).

Each of the three false claims begins with, 'If we say . . .' (verses 6, 8, 10).

FALSE CLAIM 1

The false teachers claimed that it is possible to have fellowship with God, to know him as Saviour and Lord, and continue to live 'in darkness'. It is possible that John is himself highlighting the absurdity of the claim of these false teachers to have fellowship with God. 'You claim to have fellowship with God, but he is "light" and you are walking in darkness.'

To 'walk in darkness' is to live outside the revelation of God's character and will in Scripture (*John* 3:19–20). In practical terms, it means living in defiance of God's commandments, and one of his commandments is that we 'love one another' (*John* 13:34–35). John's response is short and sharp: If we think like this 'we lie and do not practise the truth'. Thinking like this is as absurd as claiming to love someone while living a self-pleasing life that disregards the other and all he or she holds dear.

Verse 7 suggests that the particular 'darkness' John is thinking about here is the attitude that says, 'I can have fellowship with God without needing to bother having fellowship with other Christians.' Thinking like this exposes a life that has never understood the gospel. Only when we 'walk in the light as he [that is, God] is in the light', living lives shaped by who he is and the word he has spoken, do 'we have fellowship with one another'.

Faith in the Lord Jesus Christ not only brings us into union with him, but with all who are joined to him. You cannot have Christ apart from his people. You cannot have fellowship with the Father without also having fellowship with the Father's children (John

[6]

Walking in the Light

will elaborate on this at some length later in the Letter). This is the context in which we find these glorious and deeply reassuring words, 'and the blood of Jesus his Son cleanses us from all [or 'every'] sin'. To live wilfully apart from the fellowship of God's people (in body or in spirit) is to cut oneself off from God's restoring, forgiving grace in Christ; see *Matt.* 6:12, 14–15.

John tirelessly impresses on us throughout his Letter that the Christian life is not a solitary life, but a life lived in fellowship with fellow-believers. It is, however, a glorious truth that 'the blood of Jesus his Son cleanses us from all sin' (see also *Isa.* 1:18). The 'blood of Jesus [God's] Son', his sin-bearing sacrifice, not only effects our forgiveness, it washes away the stain of our sin. The whole Bible resonates with this reassuring truth. The Lord Jesus Christ came to cleanse and deliver us from our sins, not to leave us to live contentedly in them.

FALSE CLAIM 2

The second claim of these false prophets is even more astonishing than the first. They claimed to 'have no sin'. Either they were denying that we are born with sinful natures, or they were saying that faith has eradicated sin totally from our natures. People who think this are self-deceived and 'the truth is not in' them. God's Word could not be clearer: we are born into this world with sinful natures (*Psa.* 51:5), and even the child of God, loved and forgiven, needs the help of the Holy Spirit, daily, 'to put to death the deeds of the body' (*Rom.* 8:13). Rather than deny that we have inherently sinful natures, the Christian is to 'confess' sin, that is, agree with God that our sin is wicked, ugly, and destructive, and rejoice in the knowledge that 'he is faithful and just to forgive us our sins and to cleanse us from all unrighteousness'.

John here tells us two further things about God that encourage the penitent sinner. God is 'faithful'. John is not so much highlighting God's unchangableness as his covenant faithfulness. In Jeremiah's great prophecy of the coming new covenant, the Lord himself promises, 'I will forgive their iniquity, and I will remember their sin no more' (*Jer.* 31:34). God is faithful to keep all his promises, because 'all (his) promises find their Yes in [Christ]' (*2 Cor.* 1:20). But not only is God faithful; he is also 'just'. How can

[7]

God justly forgive sin? Should he not punish sin to the utmost? Yes, and he has in his only begotten Son, Jesus Christ. God will by no means clear the guilty. But in Jesus Christ, the appointed representative Head of judgment-deserving sinners (see *Rom.* 5:12–21), God has executed his just judgment on our sin. It is because God acted justly in punishing his own beloved Son 'for us' that he can justly forgive our sins (*Rom.* 3:25–26; *2 Cor.* 5:21; *1 Pet.* 3:18). Horatius Bonar, the great nineteenth-century Scottish minister and hymn-writer, put the matter memorably:

> *Upon a life I did not live,*
> *Upon a death I did not die;*
> *Another's life, another's death,*
> *I stake my whole eternity.*

This is the gospel.

FALSE CLAIM 3

The third claim of the heretics appears to maintain that, in daily living, they did not sin. Very occasionally we meet people who say they never sin! How could anyone be so foolish and so blind? Not only were these heretics self-deceived but, by their claim, they made God 'a liar' and showed that his Word was not in them. God's Word could not be clearer: 'None is righteous, no, not one . . . all have sinned and fall short of the glory of God' (*Rom.* 3:10, 23). It is a simple test of a person's Christian profession to ask whether he agrees with what God says about him in his Word, particularly in relation to sin. What God says is deeply humbling (see *Jer.* 17:9; *Rom.* 3:10–18); but it is also wonderfully comforting, because confession brings to us the hope of forgiveness and cleansing in Christ.

3

The Glorious Gospel

*M*y little children, I am writing these things to you so that you
may not sin. But if anyone does sin, we have an advocate with
the Father, Jesus Christ the righteous. ² He is the propitiation for
our sins, and not for ours only but also for the sins of the whole world
(1 John 2:1–2).

The opening verses of chapter 2 present us with a glorious
summary of biblical religion. John Calvin says that here we
have 'the sum of almost all the gospel'. In contrast with the false
prophets who were saying that sin does not really matter, John tells
us the lengths to which God has gone to set us free from the guilt,
stain, power and curse of sin. John never forgets that he is writing
as a pastor to God's people. He affectionately calls them his 'little
children'.

CHRIST OUR ADVOCATE

He first reminds us of God's ultimate purpose for our lives, 'that
you may not sin'. Far from taking or treating sin lightly, God's
purpose for his children is to remove sin completely from their
lives; see *Rom. 8:29; Eph. 1:4*. The new birth is but the beginning
of the Christian life; a vital and necessary beginning; but yet a beginning. When a farmer plants seed in the earth, it is the beginning, not the end of the story. He looks forward to the seed ripen-
ing into a rich harvest. So with God. To change the metaphor, the
Heavenly Sculptor's ultimate aim is to conform us to the likeness
of his Son, 'in order that he might be the firstborn among many
brothers' (*Rom. 8:29*). This is a lifelong process and will never be

realized this side of glory. And yet it is the mark of a Christian that he or she increasingly hates sin, loves righteousness and longs to be more like Christ.

Secondly, John reminds us of God's gracious and loving provision for us when we do sin, as sin we will: 'But if anyone does sin, we have an advocate with the Father, Jesus Christ the righteous.' Jesus is our 'advocate with the Father'. John uses a word that in his Gospel refers to the Holy Spirit, *parakletos* (*John* 14:16, 26; 15:26; 16:7). The word literally means someone called alongside to help. In Greek law, if you were accused of a crime, you might ask a best friend to speak in your defence. He would act as a *paracletos*. Just as the Holy Spirit is Christ's *paraclete* on earth, testifying to him as Saviour and Lord before a Christ-denying world, so Jesus Christ is our heavenly *paraclete*, the One who pleads our cause 'with the Father'. As our defence counsel, he is uniquely qualified to stand in God's presence to represent us, because he is 'Jesus Christ the righteous', the one who has fulfilled God's law perfectly on behalf of all believers.

But what is it that this righteous *paraclete* actually says in our defence? The answer is found in verse 2: 'He is the propitiation for our sins, and not for ours only but also for the sins of the whole world.'

'Propitiate' literally means to appease, to turn away wrath by the offering of a gift. If you upset or angered someone you loved, you might send them a 'peace offering' to turn away their anger. Jesus Christ is the offering that turns away God's wrath against our sin and makes us fit for his friendship. So what does Jesus Christ say in our defence? He never says that we are innocent; he always says, 'I am the propitiation for their sins.' Jesus himself is the believer's defence. His substitutionary blood-shedding on the cross exhausted God's holy wrath against our sin. He was 'obedient unto death' for us, and now, at the Father's right hand, he 'always lives to make intercession' for us (*Heb.* 7:25) by his presence as the one who has made a perfect propitiation for all our sins. It is not that a loving Son wins over a reluctant Father. Jesus Christ is the Father's gift of love to the world (*John* 3:16; *1 John* 4:10).

God is love (*1 John* 4:8); but we have already seen that God is also light, that he is morally pure and diametrically opposed to sin in all its forms. It is because God is who he is that we all need a 'propitiation for our sins'. This is why the theme song of every Christian is:

> *My hope is built on nothing less*
> *Than Jesus' blood and righteousness.*

This is our comfort when God's holy law reveals our guilt, when Satan condemns us, and when our own conscience accuses us. As Calvin so simply puts it: 'The reason why God does not impute our sins to us is because he looks on Christ the intercessor.'

Jesus is also 'the propitiation . . . for the sins of the whole world'. There is no other propitiation for sin in the whole world. Only in 'Jesus Christ the righteous' is there shelter from God's all-consuming wrath against sin. As Peter declared to the Jewish Council, 'There is salvation in no one else, for there is no other name under heaven given among men by which we must be saved' (*Acts* 4:12).

4

Obedience Matters

A *nd by this we know that we have come to know him, if we keep his commandments.* ⁴ *Whoever says 'I know him' but does not keep his commandments is a liar, and the truth is not in him,* ⁵ *but whoever keeps his word, in him truly the love of God is perfected. By this we may know that we are in him:* ⁶ *whoever says he abides in him ought to walk in the same way in which he walked* (1 John 2:3–6).

L ater, in Chapter 5, verse 13, John tells us the main reason why he wrote this letter. He wanted to assure his 'little children' of their standing in Christ. False prophets (4:1) were unsettling them. They appeared to be saying something like this: 'You cannot be real Christians; you haven't experienced what we have. We "know" God; we have had a special experience, and until you do, you cannot "know" God.' We hear similar comments today: 'If you don't belong to our church, you don't belong to Christ.' 'If you have not had this special experience, your Christian profession is suspect.' As a loving pastor, John is deeply concerned to reassure his 'little children' that they truly are Christ's. He does so by highlighting certain 'tests of a genuine faith'.

In verses 3–6, John highlights the 'moral test'. He is reiterating what he heard from Christ himself (see *John 14:15, 21, 23; 15*:10). John wants his beloved children, and us, to be absolutely clear that where there is a true, saving knowledge of God, there will be a heart obedience to his commandments (verse 3).

The practical evidence of authentic saving faith is a lifestyle shaped by God's commandments. Just as the Saviour himself came not to abolish the law but to fulfil it (*Matt.* 5:17), so the Christian believer 'delight(s) in the law of God in [the] inner being' (*Rom.*

7:22). A man's wife knows that he loves her, not so much by the fine words he speaks, but by his unfailing desire to please her and to honour her. True knowledge of God has moral implications. God is pleased when he sees his children keeping his commandments because they love their Saviour. So, 'Whoever says "I know him" but does not keep his commandments is a liar, and the truth is not in him.' However extravagant his profession and however astonishing his experience, if he does not keep God's commandments, he is a fraud, a spiritual charlatan.

Obedience may, and often will, be costly. It was for our Lord Jesus, and it will be for all who are united to him. The same moral obedience the Holy Spirit fashioned in Christ, he also comes to fashion in the lives of all Christians. The gospel does not set us free from God's commandments; it enables us by the power of the indwelling Holy Spirit to keep them.

In contrast to those charlatans, 'whoever keeps his word, in him truly the love of God is perfected'. The love of God in our lives is 'perfected', brought to its ordained goal, when we keep his word. Does John mean here our love for God, or his love for us? If he means our love for God, then this love is 'perfected' in our all-round obedience to his word. 'The proof of love is loyalty' (John Stott). If, however, he means God's love for us, the thought would then be that God's love so captures our hearts that we make his pleasure the all-absorbing interest of our lives, and God is pleased when all we are is shaped and styled by his Word (*John* 14:21). John has a habit of writing with 'double meanings', probably expecting us to see that our interpretation is not a matter of *either/or*, but of *both/and*.

In verses 5b–6, John personalizes his argument, 'By this we may be sure that we are in him: whoever says he abides in him ought to walk in the same way in which he walked.' 'In him' is the New Testament's most common way of describing a Christian. Faith takes us 'into Christ'. Baptism is 'into the name of the Father, the Son and of the Holy Spirit' (*Matt.* 28:19). Here John tells us that if we truly are in Christ and 'abide in him', then we will 'walk in the same way in which he walked'. The hallmark of our Lord Jesus' earthly life was glad, submissive obedience to his Father (*John* 6:38; *Heb.* 10:7). He had not come to abolish God's law but to

[13]

fulfil it (*Matt.* 5:17), and in fulfilling it to 'fulfil all righteousness' (*Matt.* 3:15). So, just as a branch is grafted on to a tree and becomes part of the tree, bearing the tree's fruit, so everyone who is united to Christ possesses the life of Christ and is being conformed to his likeness (*John* 15:5; *Rom.* 8:29; *2 Cor.* 3:18).

In practice this will mean making Jesus' priorities our priorities (*John* 5:30); sharing his compassion for the lost (*Matt.* 9:36–38); refusing to yield an inch where God's truth is at stake (*John* 18:37); and living to glorify God in all we are and do (*John* 17:1–5).

If satan should buffet.
Christ has regenace my helpless state
and shed his own blood.

walk as Jesus walked

5

The New Commandment

*B eloved, I am writing you no new commandment, but an old
commandment that you had from the beginning. The old commandment is the word that you have heard. [8] At the same time, it is
a new commandment that I am writing to you, which is true in him
and in you, because the darkness is passing away and the true light
is already shining. [9] Whoever says he is in the light and hates his
brother is still in darkness. [10] Whoever loves his brother abides in the
light, and in him there is no cause for stumbling. [11] But whoever hates
his brother is in the darkness and walks in the darkness, and does not
know where he is going, because the darkness has blinded his eyes*
(1 John 2:7–11).

John continues in these verses to highlight the marks of true, as
distinct from counterfeit, faith. In 2:3–6 we saw that authentic
faith is a deeply moral faith, a faith that is shaped and styled by
God's commandments. Now John tells us that alongside obedience
to God's commands a second mark of true faith is love for God's
people.

The 'new commandment' (verse 7) which is yet 'an old commandment' is most probably *John* 13:34–35. Jesus told his disciples
that the mark of the new age would be that they love one another
as he has loved them. The commandment is 'old' because they had
it 'from the beginning', that is from the beginning of their following the Saviour. It was from Jesus and his apostles that they had
'heard' this commandment. But it is also a 'new' commandment,
probably because Jesus had brought *new-covenant* newness to this
age-old commandment. He gave it a new depth and quality (*John*
10:11). The commandment to love one another was brought to new
perfection in the life, and supremely the death, of the Lord Jesus

[15]

Christ. In him we see the truth of brotherly love in all its astonishing, sacrificial glory. But, this new commandment of brotherly love is also seen 'in you'!

John is ministering pastoral reassurance to his 'little children'. He is assuring them that he sees one of the principal marks of saving grace in their lives. The false teachers were telling them that they had not yet arrived. John is assuring them that they have, because they love the brotherhood (*1 Pet.* 2:17). Christians are to be walking advertisements for the gospel, showing in our love for one another the transforming power of the Spirit of Christ in our lives. Love, for Christ and the people of Christ, is the distinguishing mark of the new age inaugurated by Christ. This is what John is telling us in verse 8b. This present age, characterized by 'darkness' and rebellion against God and his Word, is in the process of 'passing away', while 'the true light is already shining'. Jesus himself is the true light (*John* 1:9). He is the final and perfect revelation of God's love. The darkness has not yet fully passed away, but there is nothing more certain than that it will. The true light is already shining and one day it will irradiate a new heavens and a new earth, the home of righteousness (*2 Pet.* 3:13). If, then, Jesus is the true light and, as the true light, is supremely marked by his sacrificial love for sinners, 'Whoever says he is in the light and hates his brother is still in darkness', while 'Whoever loves his brother abides in the light' (verses 9–10). Like produces like. Whoever claims to be 'in Christ', but does not love his brothers, is a 'liar' (4:20) and is still in the darkness.

Brotherly love is a command of our Lord Jesus Christ. It is not a suggestion to consider or an optional extra to tack on to our Christian lives. Nor is doctrinal orthodoxy a substitute for brotherly love. Love for 'all the saints' (*Eph.* 1:15) is a Christian birthmark. Indeed, we are to love one another 'as Christ loved us and gave himself up for us, a fragrant offering and sacrifice to God' (*Eph.* 5:2). This will make us 'imitators of God, as beloved children' (*Eph.* 5:1).

Brotherly love transcends all denominational groupings. It is to be as wide as the world and as deep as Calvary. Such is the grace of brotherly love that it shows that we 'abide in the light', that we live in fellowship with Christ, and that in us 'there is no cause for

stumbling' (verse 10b). This is remarkable. John is possibly saying that if we love one another, the light of God's truth so illu-
minates our ways that we do not become causes of stumbling for
other Christians. Christ-like love 'is patient and kind . . . it is not
arrogant or rude. It does not insist on its own way' (*1 Cor.* 13:4–5).
Love illumines the way ahead.

In contrast, 'whoever hates his brother is in the darkness, and
does not know where he is going, because the darkness has blinded
his eyes'. Hating the people we say are our brothers, our fellow
believers, exposes the emptiness and self-delusion of our Christian
profession. Whatever we might say with our lips, our lives reveal
that we are still 'in the darkness' and the darkness actively blinds
our eyes (verse 11b), twisting and distorting our understanding of
what is good and right. The absence of brotherly love is telling
evidence of an unrenewed, unsaved life. When we handle something our fingerprints mark it. When God savingly touches a life,
he leaves his 'fingerprints' all over it. Are his 'fingerprints' on your
life?

6

Children, Young Men and Fathers

*I am writing to you, little children, because your sins are forgiven
for his name's sake. [13] I am writing to you, fathers, because you
know him who is from the beginning. I am writing to you, young
men, because you have overcome the evil one. I write to you, children, because you know the Father. [14] I write to you, fathers, because
you know him who is from the beginning. I write to you, young men,
because you are strong, and the word of God abides in you, and you
have overcome the evil one* (1 John 2:12–14).

John wants his 'little children' to be in no doubt as to his confidence in their standing in Christ. He continues to assure them
that he believes, whatever these false teachers are saying, that
they truly are God's children. He mentions three groups of people
in these verses: 'little children' (verse 12 – 'children' in verse 13);
'fathers' (verses 13, 14); and 'young men' (verses 13, 14). Some
have suggested that these are not age groups but stages of spiritual
development. That is possible. However, in 2:1 John has spoken
of the whole congregation as his 'little children' (see also 2:28) and
in 2:18 as 'children'. It seems better to see John as addressing first
the whole congregation ('Little children' and 'children'), and then
the 'fathers', the older, more mature believers, and then the 'young
men', the younger, less mature believers.

John makes six statements: the first three using the words, 'I am
writing to you', and the second three, 'I write to you', or better, 'I
have written to you'.

He addresses first the whole congregation, his 'little children'
('children' in verse 13). These hard-pressed believers needed much
encouragement and reassurance. John tells them two things calculated to provide precisely that.

1. He assures them that their sins 'are forgiven for his name's sake'. Forgiveness is the first great blessing of the gospel. God no longer holds our sin against us because Jesus Christ is the 'propitiation for our sins' (see 2:2). God fully and freely forgives all our sin 'for his [Jesus'] name's sake'. With this assurance, the Christian can face every trial, every disappointment, every calamity. Come what may, through faith in the Lord Jesus, God has forgiven all our sin.

2. John also assures them that they 'know the Father' (verse 13), that they truly are God's children. Whatever these 'higher-life' false teachers were insinuating, John assures his 'children' that God is their Father, they 'know', that is love, him. The greatest antidote to the false teaching that continually afflicts the Church is knowing that, for Jesus' sake, God has fully forgiven all our sin and made us his children.

Having addressed the church in general, John now addresses the 'fathers' within the church. The 'fathers' are the wiser, more mature, well-proved men and women (probably older as well) in the congregation, including its leaders. John says exactly the same thing to these 'fathers' in verses 13 and 14, that they have known 'him who is from the beginning'. Like the church as a whole, they 'know' the Father (see verse 13b), but as 'fathers' they know more deeply 'him who is from the beginning'. This possibly refers to the Lord Jesus Christ, see 1:1 and *John* 1:1. The false teachers were denying that he was from the beginning (see 4:1–2), but the Scriptures are adamant that he was in the beginning with God. It is significant that John singles out this particular characteristic of these 'fathers'. The great purpose of the gospel is to bring us to know God (see *John* 17:3) and growing in the knowledge of God is the mark of a healthy Christian (*2 Pet.* 3:18).

But how do we grow in the knowledge of God? The Bible gives us a full answer to this question: By praying for the Spirit of wisdom and revelation so that we will know God better (*Eph.* 1:17); by reading God's Word faithfully; by listening to God's Word eagerly; by obeying his Word diligently (*Psa.* 119:100); by seeking him in prayer earnestly; by sharing in wholehearted fellowship with his people (*Eph.* 3:18–19).

Thirdly, John addresses the 'young men' (verses 13 and 14). This second group within the church probably comprises recent converts. In encouraging them, John reminds them that they are not only children of God but soldiers for Christ. The Christian life is a battle (see *Eph.* 6:10–20), an unceasing battle with the world, the flesh and the devil. When God graciously and sovereignly brings us to faith in the Lord Jesus Christ, he brings us into a cosmic conflict. Satan is no cartoon figure; he is the enemy of God and of the people of God (*Matt.* 6:13; *1 Pet.* 5:8). This enmity was inaugurated in the garden of Eden (*Gen.* 3:15) and will only be ended when Jesus returns in power and in great glory at the end of the age finally to cast Satan and all his family (see *John* 8:42–44) into the 'lake of fire' (*Rev.* 20:10).

These 'young men' were 'strong', spiritually vigorous, God's Word was abiding in them, and they had 'overcome the evil one' (verses 13, 14). Even the youngest convert shares in Christ's triumph over the evil one (*Col.* 2:15). Union with Christ is union with the all-victorious Son of God. Satan is a defeated enemy. He continues to 'roar' (*1 Pet.* 5:8), but his head has been crushed by the risen Lord (*Gen.* 3:15). One mark of our union with Christ is that his Word abides in us, that it shapes how we think and fashions how we live. Just as our Lord Jesus vanquished Satan by the Word that abode in him (see *Matt.* 4:1–11), so that same Spirit-breathed Word continues to overcome the enemy of our souls. When Adam failed under Satan's subtle assault in Eden, it was because God's Word did not abide in him. He disregarded it and paid a terrible price. We should constantly heed the Psalmist's words: 'How can a young man keep his way pure? By guarding it according to your word . . . I have stored up your word in my heart that I might not sin against you' (*Psa.* 119:9, 11)

6

Do Not Love the World

*D*o not love the world or the things in the world. If anyone loves
the world, the love of the Father is not in him. [16] For all that is
in the world—the desires of the flesh and the desires of the eyes and
pride in possessions—is not from the Father but is from the world.
[17] And the world is passing away along with its desires, but whoever
does the will of God abides forever (1 John 2:15–17).

As a deeply concerned pastor, John includes warnings as well
as encouragements in his letter. Here he warns his 'little children' not to love 'the world'. In his Gospel, John tells us that God
'so loved the world . . .' (*John* 3:16). There 'the world' stands for
fallen, sinful humanity, a world that God amazingly loves and that
Christians, as God's children, should also love.

Here 'the world' has a darker, more sinister meaning. It stands
for an organized system that hates and openly defies God and his
Son (see *John* 15:18–25). John actually defines what he means by
'the world' in verses 16–17. The world that Christians are not to
love is the world where 'the desires of the flesh', 'the desires of the
eyes', and 'pride in possessions' dominate the horizons of life and
define the shape of life. This world Christians are to avoid, resist
and reject (see also *2 Tim.* 2:22). John is not advocating monastic
withdrawal from the world. God's people are always to be salt and
light in the world (see *Matt.* 5:13–16). What Christians are to avoid
is sharing in the sinful, God-dishonouring ambitions, desires and
activities of this fallen world. *Cliff Richard*

John's warning to his 'little children' is very solemn: 'If anyone
loves the world, the love of the Father is not in him.' Pastors who
love their congregations will speak pointedly when the occasion

demands it. One of the marks of a Christian is that he or she has come to perceive the shallow and sinful attractions of the world for what they are, attractions that are 'passing away' (verse 17). The new eyes that enable us to see in Jesus the grace of God, also enable us to see in the world the snares of the devil. It is more than possible that lying behind these verses, John has the opening verses of Genesis 3 in mind. There, God's man and woman were seduced by the very things John highlights here. Consider these three marks of a world that is even now 'passing away':

First, there are *'the desires of the flesh'*. The world John is commanding us not to love is the world where selfish craving is pursued and praised. John is not condemning pleasure; he is condemning a system that makes 'my pleasure' and not God's glory the chief pursuit of life. This was precisely Eve's downfall. She put her own desire above God's revealed will. The point is not that our bodies are evil or that sex is bad, because God gave us our bodies, made us sexual beings, and 'richly provides us with everything to enjoy' (*1 Tim.* 6:17). But when we make God's good gifts ends in themselves, we make our pleasure and satisfaction the goal of existence. In short, we make pleasure our God (see *2 Tim.* 3:4). This is the world depicted in the TV 'Soaps', in teenage, and so-called 'adult' magazines. It is a world where God, his Son, and eternity are dismissed, and selfish desire is king. The reality, and tragedy, of course, is that when God, his Son and eternity are ignored, selfish gratification leaves people unsatisfied and aching for more (see *Eccles.* 3:11). We are spiritual creatures and only the living God can satisfy our longing for life.

Second, there is *'the desires of the eyes'*. John probably has in mind here our native fallen tendency to be beguiled by appearances: 'It looks good; it must therefore be good.' We live in a superficial age, an age where outward appearance and presentation matter more than substance. This was part of Adam and Eve's downfall too. God had forbidden them to eat of the fruit of the tree of the knowledge of good and evil (*Gen.* 2:17). But when 'the woman saw that the tree was good for food, and that it was a delight to the eyes . . . she took of its fruit . . .' (*Gen.* 3:6). The world of advertising in particular is geared to seduce us through images that bypass our minds and beguile our eyes. John warns us to beware of this seduction. All that glitters is not gold!

Third, there is *'pride in possessions'*. The world Christians are not to love is the world that makes a man's life to 'consist in the abundance of his possessions' (*Luke* 12:15), that says, 'I am what I am, not by the grace of God, but by my own achievements, and here they are.' Jesus himself counsels us not to 'lay up treasures on earth where moth and rust destroy and where thieves break in and steal', but to lay up 'treasures in heaven, where neither moth nor rust destroys and where thieves do not break in and steal. For where your treasure is, there your heart will be also' (*Matt.* 6:19–21).

It is possible that John is also thinking here of *Gen.* 3. The word translated 'possessions', can be translated 'life' (as in the AV). In the Garden, Eve saw 'that the tree was to be desired to make one wise' (*Gen.* 3:6). She was reaching out in her pride to take possession of what she thought would enrich her life. But what she thought would make her 'wise' brought her death.

Satan never wearies of tempting us to believe that life can be found outside God's will and ways. It is little wonder that our Lord Jesus calls him 'a liar and the father of lies' and John describes him as 'the deceiver of the whole world' (*Rev.* 12:9). Satan was bold enough to try and tempt our Lord himself with these very temptations (*Matt.* 4:1–11), but to no avail.

One of sin's 'fingerprints' is its consuming passion to praise self. How rarely do we hear the greatly gifted acknowledging that every ability they possess is the gift of God's grace. Paul needed to ask the Christians in Corinth, 'What do you have that you did not receive? If then you received it, why do you boast as if you did not receive it?' (*1 Cor.* 4:7). If self-praise is a mark of a fallen, God-denying world, it is a sin that needs constantly to be put to death in everyone who professes to belong to Jesus Christ (*Rom.* 8:13).

John is not content merely to tell us not to love the world; he gives us three compelling reasons why we should not love the world.

First, *'If anyone loves the world, the love of the Father is not in him'* (verse 15). You cannot, whatever you may think, love God and the world at the same time (see *Matt.* 6:24; *James* 4:4). The fundamental issue has to do with the first commandment (*Exod.* 20:3). God will brook no rivals, and especially rivals that deny and despise him. A man who truly loves his wife does not enjoy the company and promote the interests of anyone who despises her and treats her with contempt. Perhaps it would be good to pause here and ask yourself this question: 'Is God's love truly in me?' If it is, you will not love the world.

Second, *'The world is passing away along with its desires, but whoever does the will of God abides forever.'* Robert Burns, in his poem *Tam O'Shanter,* captured precisely what John meant in the first part of verse 17:

> *But pleasures are like poppies spread,*
> *You seize the flow'r, its bloom is shed;*
> *Or like the snow falls in the river,*
> *A moment white, then melts for ever.*

It is the essence of folly to love what is in the process of 'passing away' and heading for eternal oblivion.

> *Fading is the worldling's pleasure,*
> *All his boasted pomp and show.*
> *Solid joys and lasting treasures*
> *None but Zion's children know.*

John Newton,
Glorious Things of Thee are Spoken

Third, *'but whoever does the will of God abides forever'.* More positively, John highlights the glorious future that lies before 'whoever' makes God's will and not the world's ways the object of their desire. To abide forever, is to live in unending communion with God in the glory of his nearer presence (see *John* 17:3).

Once again God's Word confronts us with two ways to live. There is a broad way, apparently spacious and inviting, but that leads to destruction. And there is a narrow way, apparently hard and uninviting, but that leads to life (read *Psa.* 1; *Matt.* 7:13–14). John is warning his readers to choose the narrow way that leads to life.

8

Beware of Antichrists

Children, it is the last hour, and as you have heard that anti-christ is coming, so now many antichrists have come. Therefore we know that it is the last hour. [19] They went out from us, but they were not of us; for if they had been of us, they would have continued with us. But they went out, that it might become plain that they all are not of us. [20] But you have been anointed by the Holy One, and you all have knowledge. [21] I write to you, not because you do not know the truth, but because you know it, and because no lie is of the truth. [22] Who is the liar but he who denies that Jesus is the Christ? This is the antichrist, he who denies the Father and the Son. [23] No one who denies the Son has the Father. Whoever confesses the Son has the Father also. [24] Let what you heard from the beginning abide in you. If what you heard from the beginning abides in you, then you too will abide in the Son and in the Father. [25] And this is the promise that he made to us—eternal life. [26] I write these things to you about those who are trying to deceive you. [27] But the anointing that you received from him abides in you, and you have no need that anyone should teach you. But as his anointing teaches you about everything, and is true, and is no lie—just as it has taught you, abide in him (1 John 2:18–27).

One of John's great concerns is to persuade his readers that belief and behaviour are inseparable. What you believe shapes how you live. It was because the false prophets who were troubling John's 'little children' believed that God was indifferent to sin (see 1:5–10), that they behaved with reckless disregard for his commandments (see 2:3–6). John proceeds to highlight in this section the identity of these 'antichrists' and the essence of their heretical beliefs. They manifested the same spirit of unbelief as 'the' anti-

[25]

christ who is yet to come, and whom the church had been warned about (verse 18; see *2 Thess.* 2:3–12).

John's concern is not simply to identify and expose these 'antichrists'. He is writing out of a deep concern for the spiritual good of his 'little children' (see verse 26). Error about who Jesus is and what he has done has the capacity to make us *stray*, literally cause us to *wander away from* 'the Shepherd and Overseer of [our] souls' (*1 Pet.* 2:25).

John describes the time in which these Christians were living as 'the last hour'. He is speaking theologically, not chronologically. He did not mean that within a few short hours or days the Lord Jesus Christ would return, wind up history and establish his eternal kingdom. In the New Testament, 'the last hour' is the time between the first and second comings of Christ. It is the time in which we are presently living. It is called 'the last hour' because God has only one more appointment on his calendar to fulfil before Christ returns!

Since the Lord's ascension, we have been living on the edge of eternity. One of the signs that this present age is indeed 'the last hour' is the presence of 'antichrists'. Jesus warned us of the coming of 'false christs and false prophets' (*Matt.* 24:24). Similarly John speaks of 'antichrists'.

One of Satan's tactics in his futile quest to destroy Christ's church is to infiltrate the church with 'angels of light' (see *2 Cor.* 11:14). In this section John gives them a name that highlights who they are and what they are about. Who are these 'antichrists'? They are not demons but people. John tells us a number of significant things about them.

First, *they had once been part of the church*: 'They went out from us' (see verse 19). They began life inside the church, and for a time gave the impression that they truly were united to Christ. But they abandoned the fellowship of Christ's people and so showed that they had never been truly converted. John's language is blunt, 'They went out from us, but they were not of us.' They had never truly been part of Christ's church, 'for if they had been of us, they would have continued with us'. For the New Testament, continuance is the test of reality. Jesus warned his disciples that only 'the one who endures to the end will be saved' (*Matt*.24:13).

The letter to the Hebrews was written to Christians, some of whom were contemplating leaving Christ and returning to Judaism. The writer warns them again and again against the folly and danger of turning back from Christ: 'How shall we escape if we neglect such a great salvation . . . we are [God's] house if indeed we hold fast our confidence and our boasting in our hope . . . For we share in Christ, if indeed we hold our original confidence firm to the end' (*Heb.* 2:3; 3:6, 14). Even more solemnly, the writer warns them that 'it is impossible to restore again to repentance those who have once been enlightened, who have tasted the heavenly gift, and have shared in the Holy Spirit, and have tasted the goodness of the word of God and the powers of the age to come, if they then fall away, since they are crucifying once again the Son of God to their own harm and holding him up to contempt' (*Heb.* 6:4–6).

None of this suggests that true believers can lose their salvation. These verses, however, are solemn reminders to us that false-hearted professors can appear to be true-hearted believers. One distinguishing feature between the true and the false is that the truly believing continue to the end, they do not turn back in the face of 'tribulation or persecution' (*Matt.* 13:21), or drift away, seduced by 'the cares of the world and the deceitfulness of riches' (*Matt.* 13:22).

It is undeniably true that Christians fall. Peter is a prime example. He fell from Christ badly, tragically. But he was restored. He experienced the grace of repentance and the rich grace of God's restoring love. From our side it is often impossible to know whether a professing Christian who falls was ever truly converted, or whether, like Peter and David, he has been ensnared by Satan. What we do know is that only those 'who endure to the end will be saved' (see *Matt.* 10:22; 24:13). This conviction will shape how we pray for and speak to such a person.

John is reminding us here that, at its best, the church is a mixed multitude, just as our Lord's own disciples were a mixed multitude. It is one thing to be 'in the church', and another to be 'united to Christ'. This, however, should not resign us to accepting anyone into the fellowship of Christ's church. It should make us all the more concerned to ensure, as much as we are able, that they truly have been born again of God's Spirit (see *John* 3:3–8) and give a 'credible profession of faith'. 'If they do not share our heavenly birth, they cannot share our earthly company' (John Stott).

A second characteristic of these 'antichrists' was *their denial that 'Jesus is the Christ'* (verse 22). 'Christ' means 'anointed one', 'Messiah' (the Hebrew equivalent). These 'liars' (verse 22) were denying that Jesus was God's Messiah-Son.

What was the nature of their denial? John gives us a revealing clue in 4:2–3 (see *2 John* 7). It related specifically to their refusal to believe that 'Jesus has come in the flesh'. This, says John, 'is the spirit of the antichrist'. What these 'antichrists' (false prophets and liars) denied was the foundational truth of Christ's incarnation. It was inconceivable to these men that God would ever join himself to frail flesh. It is more than probable that these 'antichrists' were infected by 'gnosticism', a form of Greek philosophy which disparaged the body and exalted the spirit.

The spirit of antichrist is as prevalent today as it was in John's day. The professing church is full of men and women who are anti-supernaturalists. They refuse to believe the plain teaching of God's Word concerning the Person of the Lord Jesus Christ. But as Benjamin Warfield, the great Princeton theologian noted, Christianity is 'unembarrassed supernaturalism'. If God's Son had not come 'in the flesh', we could never have been saved. He 'became flesh' (*John* 1:14) so that as one of us, as our representative Head, he might provide for us the righteousness that we lacked and the atonement for our sins we could never make. The gospel is profoundly supernatural, because it is the good news about God and his sovereign intervention in his Son to seek and to save the lost.

The seriousness of the antichrists' denial is that when you deny that Jesus is the Christ, come in the flesh, you 'deny the Father and the Son' (verses 22b, 23). When people deny what God has plainly revealed in his word, they are to be recognized for what they are, 'liars', 'antichrists', 'false prophets'. John's language is severe because the issues at stake are momentous. These men were denying the real Jesus and were promoting teaching that would imperil the salvation of sinners (see *John* 3:36).

The deity of Christ, his Spirit-wrought incarnation, his identity as God's Messiah-Son, are not truths that can be sacrificed for the sake of peace in the church. There can be no truly Christian unity where these truths are not embraced. It was John's deep concern for Christ's honour and the salvation and safety of his people that caused him to write as bluntly as he did. He is not being narrow-minded; he is being gospel-faithful.

In such a climate of theological error, how are Christian believers to resist being deceived and led astray?

First, *'You have been anointed by the Holy One, and you have all knowledge'* (verse 20). True Christians have been 'anointed' by the Holy One, the Holy Spirit. As the Spirit of truth he indwells every believer (*Rom.* 8:9), giving us the knowledge of the truth (verse 21).

When John says in verse 27, 'you have no need that anyone should teach you', he does not mean that Christians do not need spiritual teachers. The risen, ascended Lord has given the gifts of 'pastors and teachers' to his church, 'to equip the saints for the work of ministry, for building up the body of Christ' (*Eph.* 4:11–12). Indeed, John is himself writing to instruct his beloved children in the faith. The point he is making is that true believers, indwelt by God's Spirit of truth, do not need anyone to tell them how wrong false teaching is: they know that 'no lie is of the truth' (verse 21b). Thus the indwelling Holy Spirit sensitizes the child of God to spiritual truth and gives him an ability to discern error when it poses as truth. Is this not what the new covenant promised (see *Jer.* 31:34)? Because of the new covenant ministry of the Holy Spirit, believers share in the prophetic anointing of their risen Saviour and are not dependent on a human mediator for the knowledge of God.

Secondly, *the Holy Spirit operates in harmony with the Holy Scriptures that he inspired.* So, as we hold fast to the Scriptures we are kept on course and avoid the dangerous rocks of error that could destroy our faith (see verses 24–25). The key to spiritual stability and faithfulness lies in ensuring that God's Word abides in us.

John is here echoing Jesus' teaching in *John* 15:1–11. Not only must we hear it, we must allow it to take root in us and shape and style our whole life. This is why Peter urged his readers, 'Like newborn infants, long for the pure spiritual milk [of God's Word], that by it you may grow up to salvation' (*1 Pet.* 2:2), and why the

Psalmist declared, 'I have stored up your word in my heart, that I might not sin against you' (*Psa.* 119:11). God's Spirit-inspired truth arms our hearts and minds against false teaching and gives us an 'instinct' to see through teaching that contradicts God's Word. It should never be forgotten that the Holy Spirit works in harmony with the Holy Scriptures he inspired, never against them.

The world is full of deceivers. Even more tragically, deceivers are also found within the professing Christian church. We must cultivate a spirit of watchfulness (see *Matt.* 26:41) and 'abide in him' (verse 28). And we abide in Christ by keeping his commandments (*John* 15:10).

9

Not Ashamed

*A*nd now, little children, abide in him, so that when he appears *we may have confidence and not shrink from him in shame at his coming. [29] If you know that he is righteous, you may be sure that everyone who practises righteousness has been born of him* (1 John 2:28–29).

In verses 28–29, John sets before us one of the greatest of all encouragements to keep us from being deceived by antichrists. The end result of abiding, remaining in Christ, and not being deceived by the antichrists, is that 'when he [Christ] appears we may have confidence and not shrink from shame at his coming'. History has an ultimate destiny, the personal, visible, glorious appearing of our Lord Jesus Christ (see *Matt.* 24:29–31; *2 Thess.* 1:7–10).

History is not an endlessly repeating cycle. Nor is it destined to end by some natural cosmic cataclysm. It is heading for its God-ordained end, and that end will be signalled by Christ's appearing. This is where all of us are inexorably heading. Since this is so, our great need is to be prepared for that day, so that we will not 'shrink from him in shame at his coming'.

Think of a bride who looks forward eagerly to her wedding day. More than anything else, she wants to look her best when the day comes. Why? She wants to please her husband and gladden his heart. Only her best will do for the one who has chosen her and loved her. To arrive at the day unprepared, would be to indicate that, in some measure, love had died. Nothing more prepares the Christian to meet with Christ than abiding in him. This will mean, first, *letting Christ's Word abide in us* (verse 24).

[31]

John is telling us that we abide, continue in Christ, when we feed upon the truth, the promises, the encouragements, the warnings, and the commands of his word (*John* 15;10). If you cut yourself loose from God's Word, you will certainly drift from Christ. How diligently and faithfully do you read God's Word and seek to be shaped by its truth?

Second, *it will mean practising righteousness* (verse 29). John is highlighting here a truth that is often neglected: Since God is righteous ('he is righteous'), then those who have been 'born of him' will display the family likeness in their lives, that is, they too will be righteous. John is insistent that moral obedience to God's Word and not some kind of 'special knowledge' is the mark of a Christian (see 2:3–6).

But what does it mean to 'practise righteousness'? In the Sermon on the Mount (*Matt.* 5–7), Jesus spells out the righteous living that pleases and is acceptable to God. *Towards God*, living righteously flows from a heart-commitment to him and his Word (see *Matt.* 5:20). This may mean, as it did for Christ, experiencing the sore opposition of the world. *Towards other people*, living righteously means loving your neighbour as yourself, treating your neighbour the way God in Christ has treated you (see *Eph.* 4:25–32). *Towards yourself*, living righteously will involve living before God's face, hating all forms of hypocrisy (see *Matt.* 6:2–18), seeking with the Spirit's help to 'put to death the deeds of the body' (*Rom.* 8:13), and recollecting every day that you are a 'debtor to mercy alone'. Our Father wants all his children to face his Son's appearing confident and unashamed.

The Father's Children

*S*ee *what kind of love the Father has given to us, that we should be*
called children of God; and so we are. The reason why the world
does not know us is that it did not know him. ² *Beloved, we are God's*
children now, and what we will be has not yet appeared; but we know
that when he appears we shall be like him, because we shall see him
as he is. ³ *And everyone who thus hopes in him purifies himself as he*
is pure (1 John 3:1–3).

The opening verses of this chapter are among the most encouraging and reassuring verses in the Bible, especially for hard-
pressed Christians. John introduces us to the summit of all God's
blessings to his people in Christ: that he loves us and calls us his
children. The opening word of the chapter, 'See', summons us to
stop and contemplate and wonder at the fact that 'we should be
called children of God'. John has five things to tell us about our
adoption into God's family:

First, *the astonishing source* of our adoption: 'See what love the
Father has given to us.' John can hardly take in the wonder that
we, who by nature are 'children of [God's] wrath' (*Eph.* 2:3), have
been loved by God (literally 'lavished' with his love) and called 'his
children'. As John contemplates God's love for sinners, he invites
us to see 'what *kind* of love' this is. He uses a very expressive word
to convey the extraordinary nature of this love. The word has the
idea of seeing *'from what country'* this love is. Truly, God's love for
sinners is 'out of this world'; it is undeserved, and unsought and
yet freely given.

If a couple seek to adopt a daughter, they usually choose an
attractive child, a child who has something to commend her. But

LET'S STUDY THE LETTERS OF JOHN

what was there in any of us that was appealing or desirable? This is what John is astonished by, that 'we', rebel sinners, deserving of God's righteous condemnation, that 'we should be called children of God'. All Christians owe their salvation and all their privileges in Christ to the sovereign, undeserved love of God. This is not a distinctive of Calvinism: it is a distinctive of biblical Christianity. God's love cannot be earned or deserved; he freely lavishes it upon us. This is the bedrock of the Christian's assurance. We are 'Loved with everlasting love', and 'led by grace that love to know'.

Second, the *remarkable privilege* of our adoption: ' . . . that we should be called children of God'. As believers we not only have all our sins forgiven, but are also adopted into God's own family, and have the right to call him 'our Father', his Son our elder brother (*Heb.* 2:12), and his heaven our home (*1 Pet.* 1:4). This is no empty hope: 'and so we are'. God has indeed loved us and made us his children.

Paul expands on this thought in *Rom.* 8:15–17, where he tells us that if we are indeed God's children then we are 'heirs of God and fellow heirs with Christ, provided we suffer with him in order that we may also be glorified with him'. Here we are surely taken out of our depth. It is almost impossible for us to have any sense of what it means to be an heir of God and a fellow-heir with Christ, except that it magnifies the privilege of being a Christian. In this regard, we should carefully reflect on the qualification, 'provided we suffer with him in order that we may also be glorified with him'. If we will not bear the cross, we will never wear the crown.

Third, the *present hiddeness* of our adoption. Why does the world not recognize Christians for what they are, God's own children? It does not know who we are because it did not know who Jesus was (verse 1b). Sin, and its master Satan, blind 'the minds of unbelievers, to keep them from seeing the light of the gospel of the glory of Christ, who is the image of God' (*2 Cor.* 4:4).

Christians share in their Saviour's rejection by this world. He was the Son of God, but was 'despised and rejected by men' (*Isa.* 53:3), condemned as a common criminal, and 'cut off out of the land of the living' (*Isa.* 53:8). His glory was veiled from the sight of his persecutors, and so, in measure, is ours. We are God's children 'now', but because of our union with the Son of God, we share in his rejection by this world. Christians are like fine buildings still covered in scaffolding. Only when the buildings are completed will the scaffolding be removed and our glory be revealed.

④ Fourth, the *future perfection* of our adoption: 'We know that when he appears we will be like him.' God's ultimate purpose for every Christian is to conform us to the likeness of his Son (see *Rom.* 8:29). Nothing will deflect him from fulfilling this glorious purpose. At present we can only dimly understand what it will mean for us to be 'like him'. But 'we know that when he appears we will be like him, because we shall see him as he is'. The Christian's hope is not vague or uncertain: 'we know' we will be like him, 'because we shall see him as he is'.

God has promised that, at the end of the age, his Son will return to this earth. And when he returns and we see him as he is, glorious in the perfection of his God-Manhood, God will transform us into his likeness. He will do this, not first to secure our blessedness, but to exalt his Son and manifest him as 'the firstborn among many brothers' (*Rom.* 8:29b). This is the goal of Christian salvation.

5 Fifth, the *present activity* of our adoption (verse 3). Having focused on the privilege and glory of our adoption in Christ, John highlights what is to be the Christian's response to his new status: 'Everyone who thus hopes in him purifies himself as he is pure.' This is how every Christian believer is to live, 'everyone'. If you claim to be a child of God, then this will be a present focus in your life. To profess to be a Christian and yet be unconcerned about purifying yourself as Christ is pure would be to stand exposed as a hypocrite (see 1:6; 2:4). 'Likeness is the proof of relationship.'

The presence of this 'hope' in our hearts, the hope of seeing Christ and becoming like him, is seen in our daily commitment to personal holiness. The writer to the Hebrews urges us to 'Strive for peace with everyone, and for the holiness without which no one will see the Lord' (*Heb.* 12:14). Our Lord Jesus impressed on his hearers that only the 'pure in heart . . . shall see God' (*Matt.* 5:8).

Again and again in the New Testament we are reminded that there are two sides to Christian holiness: there is a 'putting away' and there is a 'putting on' (see *Col.* 3:1–17). Holiness, likeness to Christ, means putting to death all that is earthly in us, 'sexual immorality, impurity, passion, evil desire, and covetousness, which is idolatry'. It means putting away 'anger, wrath, malice, slander, and obscene talk from your mouth'. There will be no growth in likeness to Christ without a resolute determination, with the help of God's Spirit (*Rom.* 8:13), to do battle with indwelling sin and the pressing temptations of a godless world. But there is also a positive side to Christian holiness. We are called to 'Put on . . . as God's chosen ones, holy and beloved, compassion, kindness, humility, meekness, and patience, bearing with one another and, if one has a complaint against another, forgiving each other; as the Lord has forgiven you, so you also must forgive.' This is the present activity of every right-thinking child of God, as we await with expectation the appearing of our Saviour.

Practising Righteousness

*E*veryone who makes a practice of sinning also practises lawlessness; sin is lawlessness. *⁵ You know that he appeared to take
away sins, and in him there is no sin. ⁶ No one who abides in him
keeps on sinning; no one who keeps on sinning has either seen him or
known him. ⁷ Little children, let no one deceive you. Whoever practises righteousness is righteous, as he is righteous. ⁸ Whoever makes a
practice of sinning is of the devil, for the devil has been sinning from
the beginning. The reason the Son of God appeared was to destroy the
works of the devil. ⁹ No one born of God makes a practice of sinning,
for God's seed abides in him, and he cannot keep on sinning because
he has been born of God. ¹⁰ By this it is evident who are the children
of God, and who are the children of the devil: whoever does not practise righteousness is not of God, nor is the one who does not love his
brother* (1 John 3:4–10).

The New Testament is insistent that one of the principal
marks of the new birth is righteous, God-honouring, living
(see 2:29): 'Everyone who practises righteousness has been born
of him.' John drives this truth home relentlessly throughout this
section of his letter. He wants his 'little children' (verse 7) to be
absolutely clear that 'no one born of God makes a practice of sinning' (verse 9). How you live reveals who and what you truly are.
The false teachers, the antichrists, who were trying to lead these
believers astray (2:26; 3:7) professed to know God, but they continued to walk in the darkness (see 1:6; 2:4). How they lived, in
open defiance of God's commandments, revealed the sinful darkness of their hearts.

It may well be that these false teachers looked the part and spoke
with passion and eloquence. The truth was that they were 'of the

devil' (verse 8). Bishop Ryle wrote that all the heresies that have afflicted the church have their origin in a defective understanding of sin. John confronts us with sin's true nature and its seriousness. 'Sin is lawlessness' (verse 4); it is a wilful, deliberate trampling on God's holy law. The person who 'makes a practice of sinning' lives in defiant rebellion against God. Lawlessness is not merely the result of sin; it belongs to the essence of what sin is, rebellion against the living God. Christians are not sinless (see 1:8–10); but John is telling us that Christians do not make sinning a 'practice'. John could not be more emphatic about this: 'No one who abides in him keeps on sinning'; 'no one who keeps on sinning has either seen him or known him'; 'Whoever makes a practice of sinning is of the devil'; 'no one born of God makes a practice of sinning . . . he cannot keep on sinning . . .'

Two questions arise here: First, *what does John mean?* We know he cannot mean that Christians do not sin (see 1:8–10; 2:1–2). Nor does he mean that Christians may not sin badly. The examples of David's adultery and complicity in murder (*2 Sam.* 11) and Peter's cowardly denying of his Lord (*Matt.* 26:69–75) highlight the depths to which true believers can sink. Rather John is impressing on us that the gospel of our Lord Jesus Christ not only changes our 'state', it transforms our 'nature'. In *Rom.* 6:4 Paul declares that believers have died to sin and no longer live in it, through our union with Christ in his death (which was a death to sin, *Rom.* 6:10). More than that, we have been united to him in his resurrection, that 'we too may walk in newness of life' (*Rom.* 6:4; *Col.* 3:1–17). In Christ we have been sanctified (*1 Cor.* 1:2). God has 'delivered us from the domain of darkness and transferred us into the kingdom of his beloved Son' (*Col.* 1:13). To continue, then, to live after you profess faith in Christ as you did before you professed faith in Christ is to show that you never truly believed in God's Son. Yes, Christian believers sin, but sin is not the ruling pattern in their lives.

Through our union with Christ we have died, not only to sin's guilt, but also to its dominating, reigning power (see *Rom.* 6:1–14). Listen to Paul: 'If anyone is in Christ, he is a new creation. The old has passed away; behold the new has come' (*2 Cor.* 5:17). You cannot be united to Christ and keep on sinning. As children of God we cannot go on sinning as before, because we have been united to the Christ who died to sin and 'was raised from the dead by the glory of the Father [so that] we too might walk in newness of life' (*Rom.* 6:4). It is not only unthinkable that a Christian should make a practice of sinning (verse 4), it is inconceivable that he should do so.

A second question inevitably follows: *Why is it unthinkable and inconceivable?* John gives us a number of reasons.

First, 'Whoever makes a practice of sinning is of the devil' (verse 8). The mark of the devil is 'sin', lawlessness, rebellion against God and his Word, a rebellion that has been 'from the beginning'. No matter how insistent someone is that he is a Christian, if he 'makes a practice of sinning' (verse 8a), he shows that his real father is the devil, not God.

Second, 'The reason the Son of God appeared was to destroy the works of the devil' (verse 8b). On the cross, by the sin-bearing, sin-atoning death of his Son, God 'disarmed the rulers and authorities and put them to open shame, by triumphing over them in him' (*Col.* 2:15). Satan may yet continue to trouble the child of God, but his power over us has been forever broken. God 'has delivered us from the domain of darkness and transferred us into the kingdom of his beloved Son, in whom we have redemption, the forgiveness of sins' (*Col.* 1:13–14).

By his representative perfect life, sin-bearing death and triumphant resurrection, our Lord Jesus Christ has secured the present and everlasting blessedness of believers (see *Rom.* 5:18–21). And now, by his Spirit, he comes to accomplish in our lives the great salvation he has won for us, enabling us to 'put to death . . . what is earthly in us . . . [and] to put on, as God's chosen ones, holy and beloved, compassion, kindness, humility, meekness, and patience . . .' (*Col.* 3:5,12f). Not only then is it inconceivable that as Christians we could want to continue living lawlessly in rebellion against the Saviour who came 'to destroy the works of the devil', it is actually impossible for us to do so. Why? Because this sin-conquering Saviour indwells us in his Holy Spirit, and the great ministry of the Holy Spirit in our lives is to make us like Christ, THE Holy One.

It may be worth pausing here to make two points: (1) The devil is no theological figment of the imagination. He is a powerful spiritual being, who behaves 'like a roaring lion, seeking someone to devour' (*1 Pet.* 5:8; see *Eph.* 6:10–12). (2) The 'works of the devil' can be 'refined' as well as gross. Anything that blinds men and women to the truth of God's glorious Saviour-Son is a 'work of the devil'.

Third, 'No one born of God makes a practice of sinning, for God's seed abides in him, and he cannot keep on sinning because he has been born of God' (verse 9). When God plants the 'seed' of new life in our souls at the new birth (*John* 3:3–8; *1 Pet.* 1:22–23), he gives us a new heart, with new affections and new desires. The seed of new life, which is God's own life in our souls (verse 9), reveals itself in God-like living, producing in our lives a harvest of righteousness.

John is absolutely emphatic: the child of God 'cannot keep on sinning because he has been born of God' (verse 9b), not that Christians do not sin, but that sin is no longer the pattern that shapes their lives. It is an unwelcome, unholy intruder, not an honoured guest. Your attitude to sin will tell you, and others, whether your Christian profession is genuine or false.

John concludes and sums up his argument in verse 10. There are but two kinds of people in the world, 'the children of God' and 'the children of the devil'. There is an echo here of *Gen.* 3:15. The fault-line that divides our world is not racial and economic; it is spiritual and theological. Everyone everywhere belongs to one of these two families. And, John tells us, it is 'evident' who belongs to God's family and who belongs to the devil's family: 'Whoever does not practise righteousness is not of God, nor is the one who does not love his brother.' For the New Testament, the credibility of the Christian's profession of faith in Christ as Saviour and Lord is seen in the transformed lifestyle which the new birth initiates in our lives. For John this transformed lifestyle has two main features: the practice of righteousness (as we have already seen) and the love of fellow believers.

Notice that John is once again echoing the teaching of Jesus: 'A new commandment I give to you, that you love one another: just as I have loved you, you also are to love one another. By this all people will know that you are my disciples, if you have love for one another' (*John* 13:34–35). What this will mean in practice is spelled out by Paul in *1 Cor.* 13:4–7 and *Eph.* 4:31–5:2. Love at its heart is selfless service. Love 'does not insist on its own way' (*1 Cor.* 13:5). On the contrary, love lays down its life to seek and secure the good of others (see *Eph.* 5:25–27; *1 John* 3:16–18). To claim to be a child of the God who is love (4:7–8, 16), and yet not love your brother, is to show that your true 'parent' is not God but the devil. This should deeply humble us and challenge us.

Loving One Another

*F*or this is the message that you have heard from the beginning,
that we should love one another. [12] We should not be like Cain,
who was of the evil one and murdered his brother. And why did he
murder him? Because his own deeds were evil and his brother's righteous. [13] Do not be surprised, brothers, that the world hates you. [14] We
know that we have passed out of death into life, because we love the
brothers. Whoever does not love abides in death. [15] Everyone who
hates his brother is a murderer, and you know that no murderer has
eternal life abiding in him. [16] By this we know love, that he laid down
his life for us, and we ought to lay down our lives for the brothers.
[17] But if anyone has the world's goods and sees his brother in need,
yet closes his heart against him, how does God's love abide in him?
[18] Little children, let us not love in word or talk but in deed and in
truth (1 John 3:11–18).

John now picks up his closing statement in verse 10 and explains
what it means to love our brothers in Christ. He relentlessly
impresses on us that the tests of true faith are *theological* (what we
believe), *moral* (how we live) and *social* (how we love).

Thus far he has majored, though not exclusively, on the test of
'righteousness' – Has the new birth produced the practice of righteousness in our lives? Are our lives, in other words, shaped and
fashioned by God's commandments (see 2:3–4)? John turns now to
focus on a second test of true faith: 'We know that we have passed
out of death into life, because we love our brothers. Whoever does
not love abides in death' (verse 14).

John could not be more categorical. The absence of love reveals
the absence of faith and the solemn fact that we yet 'abide in death',
in a state of separation from God, under his curse, and facing the

nightmare prospect of hell. If God is love (4:8), it is inconceivable that his spiritual children would not, in some measure, share his likeness.

John has much to tell us about Christian love in this section:

First, *love is a command Christians are bound to obey* (see verse 11). As we noticed above, John is clearly thinking here about Jesus' own teaching, 'the message that you heard from the beginning' (see *John* 13:34-35). There Jesus calls the love that is to mark indelibly the lives of his disciples 'a new commandment'. It was a 'command' to obey, not a suggestion to consider. And it was 'new', not because God's people did not love one another before the coming of Jesus, but because with his coming love was given a new pattern, based on his example – 'Love one another just as I have loved you', selflessly and sacrificially.

Christian love is not an emotion that rises or falls with changing circumstances and inclinations. It is never to be a hostage to our fluctuating emotions. This accounts for John's solemn warning in verse 12. Instead of following verse 11 with verse 16, John pauses to issue an illustrated warning: 'We should not be like Cain . . .' The story of Cain is found in *Gen.* 4. It is a tragic story. Out of jealousy, Cain murdered his brother Abel and spent the rest of his life 'away from the presence of the LORD' (*Gen.* 4:16).

Why does John introduce such an extreme example? Perhaps for two reasons: (1) Cain and Abel were brothers! They had the same biological parents, but were from different spiritual families (see verse 10). His attitude to his brother Abel revealed that Cain was a child of the devil, he was 'of the evil one' (verse 10).

It is an undeniable and solemn fact that throughout history there have been people who have been 'in' the church, but not 'of' the church. Judas belonged to the Twelve, but his actions betrayed him as a child of the devil. It is only too possible to be 'in' the fellowship of Christ's church and yet not be savingly united to Christ. We can never be too often reminded, 'You will recognize them by their fruits' (*Matt.* 7:20)

(2) John's example is extreme, but he is highlighting the ability of the human heart to sin deceitfully (see *Jer.* 17:9). We should never underestimate the sinful potential lurking in our hearts. John raises the example of Cain because he knows how easily jealousy

can creep on us and cause resentment and worse to be harboured in our hearts. Cain did not 'put to death the deeds of the body' (*Rom.* 8:13), but allowed them to grow like wild weeds until they consumed him, and he murdered his brother. This is a warning no Christian should lightly ignore. We should take our Saviour's words to heart, 'Pray that you may not enter into temptation' (*Luke* 22:46).

We should also 'not be surprised' if the world hates us (verse 13). The world in its native hostility to God hates all those who are identified with him. Just as Cain hated and then killed his brother Abel, so the world never tires of hating, and at times killing, men and women of faith like Abel. This is just how things are because of the believer's union with Christ. He forewarned his disciples of the inevitable antagonism of the world (see *John* 15:18–25); and Peter urged his readers, 'Beloved, do not be surprised at the fiery trial when it comes upon you to test you, as though something strange were happening to you' (*1 Pet.* 4:12).

Second, *the love Christians are to practise is seen in selfless sacrificial service* (see verse 16). Jesus is the model and exemplar of what it means to love one another. 'By this we know love, that he laid down his life for us, and we ought to lay down our lives for the brothers.' Here John highlights a pattern that is imbedded throughout God's Word: God's commands to us are rooted in the wonder of his grace to us in his Son.

What constrains obedience is not merely the fact that God himself commands us, though that would be a sufficient motive. Being the God of grace that he is, our Father seeks always to give us further powerful reasons for obedience. We see this pattern in *Exod.* 20:1–17 when God, through Moses, gave his people the Ten Commandments. Before he says, 'You shall have no other gods before me' (verse 3), he says, 'I am the LORD [the covenant Lord] your God, who brought you out of the land of Egypt, out of the house of slavery.' What a glorious incentive to obedience! God had rescued and redeemed them; he was their God, the covenant Lord who had made them his people.

John presents us with this same pattern in verse 16. Our Lord Jesus Christ 'laid down his life for us'. For us he became a sin-bearing sacrifice. For us he experienced the God-forsakenness of the cross (*Matt.* 27:46) that we might be rescued from the hell our sins deserved and reconciled to God. Loving our brothers as Christ loved us could mean making the ultimate sacrifice to secure their good (see *John* 15:13).

Once again we see that the Christian family life is to imitate the divine family life. If our loving commitment to our Christian brothers and sisters is less than it should be, it can only mean that we have lost sight of the wonder of the cross. The cross is not only the centrepiece of the Christian faith, it is the pulse-beat of the Christian life. We never graduate beyond it. Where love is failing, our great need is not so much to be exhorted to love, but to be re-acquainted with the Saviour's selfless sacrifice for sinners.

Third, John is insistent that *Christian love is seen in the practical sharing of our God-given resources with needy brothers* (verses 17–18). He is concerned that his little children understand that Christian love is not merely fine sounding words (verse 18). He is probably thinking of the false prophets (4:1) whose 'love' was devoid of practical care and selfless sharing.

These are deeply searching words. If believers truly are God's family, then how can we close our hearts and deprive anyone in the family of basic needs? Christian love, like Christian faith (see *James* 2:14–26) does not hoard goods, but shares them with needy saints (see *Acts* 2:44–45; 4:32). As Paul reminded the Christians in Corinth, 'What do you have that you did not receive?' (*1 Cor.* 4:7). Everything we have, we have from God as gifts of his grace. Just as spiritual gifts are to be used above all 'to serve one another' (*1 Pet.* 4:10); so the earthly goods God gives us are to be shared with those in need.

John is not advocating some kind of primitive socialism; he is encouraging Christ-like behaviour. Love gives and gives sacrificially (*Eph.* 5:25). Although he highlights the giving and sharing of this 'world's goods', we can hardly limit a brother's 'needs' to this. The gospel summons us to share our time, our friendship, and much else besides, with our needy brothers and sisters. As ever the example we are to follow is that of our Lord Jesus who unwearyingly gave himself to minister to the needs of others (see *Matt.* 9:35–36). Supremely it is his selfless sacrifice for us that shapes and inspires the practice of love for others.

Fourth, John echoes Jesus' teaching that *the presence and practice of Christian love in our lives is a sure indication of the presence of God's salvation in our lives* (verses 14–15; see *John* 13:34–35). The New Testament is insistent that wherever the gospel takes saving root it will reveal itself unmistakably. The faith that brings us from death into life, from alienation from God and the sentence of death, is always accompanied by life-giving power – it does not, and cannot, remain alone (see *James* 2:14–26).

John has already told us that keeping God's commandments is one of the fruits of saving, life-giving faith (2:3–6); now he tells us that love for the brothers is another fruit of a saved life. John's description of conversion is both dramatic and unequivocal: 'We have passed out of death into life' (verse 14). Spiritual death is the natural condition of everyone born into our world (see *Gen.* 2:17; *Eph.* 2:1,5; *Psa.* 51:5). This condition is not simply the fruit of our personal sin and rebellion against God (*Rom.* 3:23); it is the result of our union with Adam, our first and fallen covenant head (see *Rom.* 5:12–21; *1 Cor.* 15:21–22). Our death in sin, however, has been reversed by Jesus Christ. Just as Adam dragged us all down into alienation and death, so Jesus Christ lifts us up to fellowship and life (see *Rom.* 6:4–5, 11).

This is why it is impossible for a Christian to go on living as he or she once did. Union with Christ brings us into possession of the 'life' of Christ (*John* 11:25; 14:6). One of the fruits of this new life is love for our fellow believers. Faith unites us to Christ and to his church; it brings us into the fellowship of the family of the living God (see 3:1–2). It should not surprise us, then, that the New Testament very often describes the evidence of saving faith in terms of a new relationship with God's people (see *Acts* 2:42; *Col.* 3:12–14). Jesus was adamant that, 'By this all people will know that you are my disciples, if you have love for one another' (*John* 13:35).

For John, the absence of love for our Christian bothers is a sure sign that we yet 'abide in death' (verse 14), separated from the life of God, under his curse and judgment. In the context here, to 'hate' your Christian brother means not to 'love' him. There is no middle ground. If we are not loving our brothers, seeking their good to the point of laying down our lives for them, then we are hating them. We need to see through the myth of neutrality, as if it were possible for a Christian believer truly to be a Christian while refusing to love someone God loves and for whom Christ died. John's words are deeply disturbing: 'Everyone who hates his brother is a murderer, and you know that no murderer has eternal life abiding in him.' Saving faith brings us into union with Christ, the God who is love. Likeness is the evidence of belonging. That is something that we should ponder often.

13

God Is Greater Than Our Hearts

By this we shall know that we are of the truth and reassure our heart before him; [20] *for whenever our heart condemns us, God is greater than our heart, and he knows everything* (1 John 3:19–20).

John's purpose in writing this letter was to assure his beloved children that they had 'eternal life' (5:13). Lack of assurance is a crippling spiritual sickness. God wants his children to know that they truly are his. Yet there are times when 'our heart condemns us' (verse 20) and we need God's reassurance that we truly are his children.

It is difficult to know whether the opening phrase in verse 19, 'By this we shall know', looks back or forward. The same phrase in verse 16 looks forward, but in 4:6 it looks back. John could be looking forward and encouraging us with the great truth that even when our hearts do condemn us, God is greater than our hearts. The verdict that ultimately counts is not the verdict I pass on myself, but the verdict that God passes on me. And so we are to appeal from our nagging conscience to the greatness of God as our sufficient Saviour and the loving Restorer of the penitent.

In the flow of John's argument, however, it seems more likely that he is drawing a reassuring conclusion from the previous section and, in particular, verse 18. If we love our Christian brothers 'in deed and in truth', and not only 'in word or talk', then we shall know ('By this') that we are 'of the truth' (verse 19). This confidence is important for John as he seeks to assure his 'little children' of their standing in Christ. The words, 'whenever our heart condemns us', suggest that this may be a marked, and recurring, feature in the believer's life.

Our hearts condemn us legitimately and illegitimately. They condemn us rightly when we sin, and especially in this context when we neglect to love our fellow Christians as God has commanded us. But our hearts also have a way of condemning us falsely, especially when they listen to the condemning lies of the evil one, who is always seeking to turn us in upon ourselves and away from our sin-vanquishing, sin-cleansing Saviour.

How are we to reassure our hearts when they condemn us? By resting in the knowledge that the God who 'knows everything', and who is 'greater than our heart', knows that we love our fellow believers 'in deed and in truth', however weakly and less than perfectly.

The presence of love in our hearts is a manifest evidence of the new birth. John's language here echoes Jesus' encounter with Peter after the resurrection (see *John* 21:15–19). When pressed three times by Jesus with the question, 'Do you love me?', Peter appeals to Jesus' knowledge of him, 'Lord, you know everything; you know that I love you.' Like Peter, we are not to rest in our feelings, or faith, or love, or obedience, but on God who is greater than our hearts and who knows everything. John Stott captures the essence of John's teaching:

> So it is knowledge which alone can quieten the condemning heart, our own knowledge of our sincere love for others and supremely God's knowledge of our thoughts and motives. Stronger than any chemical tranquillizer is trust in our all-knowing God.

J. R. W. Stott, *The Epistles of John*
(Tyndale Press, 1964), p. 146).

What Pleases God

Beloved, if our heart does not condemn us, we have confidence before God; ²² and whatever we ask we receive from him, because we keep his commandments and do what pleases him. ²³ And this is his commandment, that we believe in the name of his Son Jesus Christ and love one another, just as he has commanded us. ²⁴ Whoever keeps his commandments abides in God, and God in him. And by this we know that he abides in us, by the Spirit whom he has given us (1 John 3:21–24).

John highlights here the blessings of an un-condemning heart. While it is true that every Christian knows the experience of a condemning heart (consider 'whenever' in verse 20), when God in his grace pacifies our hearts, certain blessings follow. First, *'we have confidence before God'* (verse 21). These are wonderful words. They picture a believer approaching God with the unaffected confidence and boldness of a little child with his father.

When we are assured that we truly are the Lord's, that the One who knows everything assures us that we are his and that he is ours, we can live before him in settled confidence. This is as far removed from pride-filled presumption as light is from darkness. Our confidence is not based on anything we are or have done, but on God's gracious acceptance of us in Christ.

Second, *'whatever we ask we receive from him'*. Is this not how a child approaches his father, always confident of his readiness to give him whatever he asks? There is, of course, an inbuilt proviso (see 5:14). No right-thinking child wants anything that is bad or displeasing to his father and no right-thinking father would ever dream of giving his child anything that was not beneficial. The perfect Son, Jesus Christ, prayed, 'not as I will, but as you will' (*Matt.* 26:39).

This is the point John is making in verse 22b. His meaning is not that our obedience to God earns us 'brownie points'; but that our obedience is evidence that our great desire in life is to do and to have only what is pleasing to our God and Saviour. Our obedience to God's commandments reveal that our will and God's will are in harmony. God's rich blessings – and answered prayer is surely one of his greatest blessings – are never rewards for services rendered, as if we could earn or merit anything from God. It is, however, God's good pleasure to honour those who honour him (see *1 Sam.* 2:30) and nothing more honours God than keeping his commandments and living to please him.

John proceeds to highlight those commands that we must obey if we are to receive from God what we ask. Strikingly, he tells us that essentially there is but one commandment, 'his commandment [singular], that we believe in the name of his Son Jesus Christ and love one another just as he has commanded us' (verse 23). God commands all people everywhere to repent and to believe in his Son (*Acts* 17:30; *John* 3:16).

To 'believe' in God's Son Jesus Christ means to receive him as Saviour and Lord (*John* 1:12), God's Anointed Prophet, Priest and King ('Christ' = Messiah, Anointed One). Saving faith is much more than notional assent. It is trusting God's Son as our only hope, resting on the perfect sufficiency of his atoning sacrifice and the perfect righteousness of his obedient life as our covenant Head (see *Rom.* 5:12–21).

But this faith in God's Son does not exist in a vacuum; it unites us to him and makes us partakers of the very life of God. This is why John writes here of one 'commandment' (singular) and yet tells us that faith in God's Son is linked inextricably to love for one another. Faith not only unites us to Christ, it initiates us into the people of Christ, the church.

These, then, are the twin birthmarks of the Christian believer: *faith in God's Son* and *love to his people*, our brothers and sisters. This is so important for John that he will later tell us that 'he who does not love his brother whom he has seen cannot love God whom he has not seen' (4:20). Indeed, this is what the Lord Jesus 'commanded us' (see *John* 13:34). The absence of love reveals the absence of faith.

All of this leads John to reiterate the truth he highlighted in 2:3–6. Who are those who 'abide in him, and he [that is, Christ] in them'? Who are those who have believed 'into Christ' and are truly God's own children? Those who keep his commandments (verse 24). John is constantly seeking to arm his 'little children' against the errors of the antichrists. The gospel is pervasively moral. God is light (1:5). Where there is no moral transformation, there is no faith in Jesus Christ (see *Eph* .2:8–10).

This is underlined by John in the closing words of verse 24. 'And by this we know that he abides in us': Christian assurance is not a matter of uncertain conjecture. Rather, 'we know'. But how do we 'know' that Christ truly dwells in us? We know 'by the Spirit whom he has given us'. The presence and work of God's Spirit in us seals to our hearts and minds the assurance 'that he abides in us' (verse 24).

Alongside the objective assurance that we keep God's commandments, and seek to live to please him (verse 22), there is the subjective or inward assurance that the Holy Spirit imparts to us. Paul wrote about this in *Rom.* 8:16: 'The Spirit himself bears witness with our Spirit that we are children of God.' This inward witness of the Spirit enables us to cry with the confidence of a little child, 'Abba! Father!' (*Rom.* 8:15). Our own spirits do bear witness that we are God's children, as we see our faith in his Son Jesus Christ and our desire to please him and keep his commandments (verses 22–23). But that often imperfect and easily-challenged assurance is indelibly confirmed to us by the inward testimony of God's own Spirit.

The Spirit does not give this assurance to those who are not believing in Christ, keeping his commandments, and seeking to please him. For the Spirit's presence in a believer's life cannot be hidden. He is the 'Holy' Spirit, whose great mission is to glorify Christ (*John* 16:14) and to conform us to his likeness (*Gal.* 5:22–23). Every Christian is indwelt by the Holy Spirit (*Rom.* 8:9–10), whose ministry in us is to reproduce what he first produced in Christ, so that Christ may be 'the firstborn among many brothers' (*Rom.* 8:29).

15

Test the Spirits

B *eloved, do not believe every spirit, but test the spirits to see whether they are from God, for many false prophets have gone out into the world. ² By this you know the Spirit of God: every spirit that confesses that Jesus Christ has come in the flesh is from God, ³ and every spirit that does not confess Jesus is not from God. This is the spirit of the antichrist, which you heard was coming and now is in the world already. ⁴ Little children, you are from God and have overcome them, for he who is in you is greater than he who is in the world. ⁵ They are from the world; therefore they speak from the world, and the world listens to them. ⁶ We are from God. Whoever knows God listens to us; whoever is not from God does not listen to us. By this we know the Spirit of truth and the spirit of error* (1 John 4:1–6).

John returns here explicitly to the theme that underlies everything he writes in this letter: the church was in danger from 'false prophets', 'antichrists' (2:18). These were men who claimed to speak from God, but who were animated by 'the spirit of the antichrist' (verse 3). We live in a similar world to John's. Our world is awash with all kinds of religions and sects, all claiming to be from God and to speak for God. Who are we to believe? How are we to distinguish between what is truly from God and what is false and from 'the spirit of the antichrist'?

First, *we are to 'test the spirits'* (verse 1). Who are these 'spirits'? They are 'false prophets'. John tells us that there are 'many' of them and they have 'gone out into the world', most probably to deceive it. John is thinking of the people he wrote about in 2:18–19. As men claim to speak and act from God, our first responsibility is to test, to examine, to scrutinize carefully what they are saying and how they are behaving.

[53]

Our minds are to be on 'red alert' as we listen to men speaking and preaching. It is only too easy to be mesmerized by powerful personalities, impressed by a preacher's eloquence or credentials, or even his appearance (see *1 Sam*.16:6–7). The test is not whether the preacher is impressive and his message attractive, but whether what he says is true. Jesus warned his disciples, 'Pay attention to what you hear' (*Mark* 4:24).

Even if men come performing miracles we are still to test them (see *Deut*. 13:1–5) and not be unthinkingly beguiled by them. This testing of the spirits is not the responsibility only of the church's leaders, though they surely have a great responsibility to do it (see *2 Tim*. 3:1–4:6). John tells us that this is the responsibility of every Christian.

Second, *we are to test the spirits particularly by what they say about Jesus Christ* (verses 2–3). This is the critical theological test the church is to apply to every preacher, teacher, and scholar. Doctrine matters. It seems likely that these 'many false prophets' denied that God's Son had 'come in the flesh'. They taught that God would never demean himself by becoming 'flesh'. But God's Son did become 'flesh' (*John* 1:14) and one of the hallmarks of true preachers, ordained by the Spirit of God, is that they 'confess that Jesus Christ has come in the flesh'. They proclaim unambiguously the truth of his incarnation, the 'becoming in flesh' of God's eternal Son. How else could God have saved sinners if his Son had not come in our flesh and, as our representative Head, fulfilled all righteousness and made atonement for sin?

John's language suggests that these false prophets not only denied the incarnation of Christ, they also denied the pre-existence of Christ. It is the 'spirit [that is, true prophet] that confesses that Jesus Christ *has come* in the flesh [that] is from God'. Bethlehem was not the beginning of God's Son, it was his appearing in our flesh: 'Before Abraham was I am'; 'In the beginning was the Word, and the Word was with God, and the Word was God. He was in the beginning with God . . . And the Word became flesh and dwelt among us . . .' (*John* 8:58; 1:1–2, 14).

Anyone who teaches that Jesus was *only* a man, a good, even great and unique man, 'is not from God'. Jesus is nothing less than incarnate God. The divine uniqueness of Jesus is a scandal to many, but it is the revealed truth of God's Word. This is why Christians can never in good conscience engage in multi-faith worship. It is not a matter of being awkward, but of being faithful to our divine and only Saviour, Jesus Christ, God's Son.

Tragically this 'spirit of the antichrist' (verse 3) is often found within the professing Christian church today. The tragedy relates not only to the huge dishonour that is brought to God's Son, but also to the spiritual peril into which it draws men and women. John, indeed the whole New Testament, is adamant, that 'there is salvation in no one else, for there is no other name under heaven given among men by which we must be saved' (*Acts* 4:12; see *John* 14:6).

Third, *we have been given the Holy Spirit to guide us into God's truth and protect us from destructive error* (verse 4). In the context of John's argument, 'have overcome them' means, 'have not been deceived by these false prophets, but have seen through their lies'.

But how do Christians 'overcome' these false teachers with their plausible but pernicious lies? Through the indwelling presence and ministry of the Holy Spirit: 'For he who is in you is greater than he who is in the world.'

There is little doubt that John is highlighting here the indwelling presence and ministry of the Holy Spirit. Jesus promised his disciples that, 'When the Spirit of truth comes [that is, at Pentecost], he will guide you into all the truth, for he will not speak on his own authority, but whatever he hears he will speak, and he will declare to you the things that are to come' (*John* 16:13). What became true in a unique sense for Christ's apostles at Pentecost also became true for every Christian believer (see *Acts* 2:1–4,38–39). Because the Holy Spirit is 'greater than he [the spirit of the antichrist] who is in the world', he is able to protect those who are 'from God'.

But how does the Spirit protect us from the antichristian lies of the 'many false prophets [who] have gone out into the world'? He does so by illumining our minds to the truth concerning our Lord Jesus Christ. Just as he inspired the holy Scriptures (*2 Tim.* 3:16; *2 Pet.* 1:20–21), so he enables our renewed minds to understand the teaching of those Scriptures.

There is, however, something more. The indwelling presence of God's own Spirit alerts us to the contaminating lies of false prophets. He is like a spiritual Geiger counter, alerting the child of God to doctrinal error, especially error concerning the Person and work of Christ. The Psalmist had real insight into this. He prayed, 'Open my eyes, that I may behold wondrous things out of your law' (*Psa.*119:18); and he declared, 'I have more understanding than all my teachers, for your testimonies are my meditation' (*Psa.* 119:99).

In verses 5–6, John contrasts the origin of these false teachers with that of true teachers, and also contrasts their respective audiences. False teachers are 'from the world'. They and their message belong to the sphere of this fallen world and, not surprisingly, the world listens to them. The message of the false teachers fits in well with the prevailing thinking of the world. It does not challenge or confront the world with its sin and rebellion against God, and so the world in its falleness 'listens to them'.

This is how it is in so many places today. False prophets, masquerading as men and women of God, proclaim a message that sits comfortably with our multi-faith, anti-supernatural, relativistic world. Biblical truths that offend are jettisoned in the name of progress and multi-faith harmony. It has even been suggested that the Church should produce a Bible that brackets all passages 'offensive' to other faiths, explaining that this is what Christians once believed – but no longer! In contrast, 'We [that is, the apostles] are from God. Whoever knows God listens to us.' This is not arrogance. John is affirming, that Christ's appointed apostles represent him and speak his Word. They did not choose Christ, he chose them (*John* 15:16) and commissioned them, 'Go . . . and make disciples of all nations . . . teaching them to observe all that I have commanded you' (*Matt.* 28:19–20).

One of the distinguishing marks of people who know God is that they listen to, believe, and embrace, apostolic teaching (see *2 Tim.* 1:13; 3:14–15; *Titus* 1:9; *Rom.* 6:17). The new birth gives us an appetite for God's truth. A refusal to listen to apostolic truth, reveals a heart that is as yet unrenewed. Jesus said, 'My sheep hear my voice, and I know them, and they follow me' (*John* 10:27). Your response to the ministry of God's Word will in large measure reveal whether you 'know God' or whether you are 'not from God'. 'By this', says John, 'we know the Spirit of truth and the spirit of error'.

Submission to Christ's Word in the apostolic Scriptures is one of the birthmarks of a child of God. The 'spirit of error', however, is characterized by a refusal to submit to the apostles' testimony to Christ. Man's reason, not God's revelation, is the final authority for the 'spirit of error'.

16

God Is Love

*B*eloved, let us love one another, for love is from God, and whoever loves has been born of God and knows God. *8 Anyone who
does not love does not know God, because God is love. *9 In this the
love of God was made manifest among us, that God sent his only Son
into the world, so that we might live through him. *10 In this is love,
not that we have loved God but that he loved us and sent his Son to
be the propitiation for our sins. *11 Beloved, if God so loved us, we also
ought to love one another. *12 No one has ever seen God; if we love
one another, God abides in us and his love is perfected in us* (1 John
4:7–12).

This is one of the most sublime passages in the New Testament.
John urges his readers to 'love one another' (verses 7 and 11),
to show in their relationships with one another the love that marks
them out as being children of the God who is love (verse 8). John
is once again pressing on us the truth that without God-like love
to our fellow Christian brothers and sisters, we expose ourselves as
religious charlatans and frauds (see verse 8).

In 3:16–18, John had shown the nature of the love that is to shape
and fashion the lives and relationships of God's children. Here
he gives us three reasons or arguments to inspire us to love one
another. Love is a command we are to obey (*John* 13:34–35), but
like all biblical commands, it is rooted in the soil of God's grace.
Who God is and what he has done for us in his Son, is what ultimately constrains obedience from the child of God. This is what
distinguishes evangelical obedience from legal obedience.

First, *we are to love one another because 'God is love'* (verses 7–8).
Not only is love 'from God', 'God is love'. It is because God is love

God Is Love

that 'whoever loves has been born of God and knows God'. God is love. This is who he is.

Three other statements in the New Testament highlight who God is: 'God is spirit' (*John* 4:24); 'God is a consuming fire' (*Heb.* 12:29); and 'God is light' (*1 John* 1:5). God is, at the same time, all of these (and much more beside). Because he is love, all he does is love. Because he is a consuming fire and light, all he does is pure and just and holy. His love is not, and cannot be, blind and indulgent, just as his justice and holiness are not, and cannot be, cold and arbitrary.

Much dishonour has been done to God, and great damage to the eternal good of sinners, by isolating God's love from his justice and holiness. The distinguishing hallmark of God's love is its unconfined and gracious nature. 'God so loved the world . . .' (*John* 3:16; 'Christian love is to be as unconfined as the sun', John Owen). Christians should love one another, then, because 'love is from God, and whoever loves has been born of God and knows God' (4:7). We have already observed that likeness is the proof of relationship. This is certainly true in the Christian faith. If we have been born of God, and like gives birth to like, then we will love one another.

This is true, and yet John writes, 'Let us love one another.' He is calling us and challenging us to be what we are, to practise the love that is native to our new nature in Christ. It is not a matter of feeling like it, but doing it. Moreover, it is absurd to claim to have been born of God and know God if we do not love our fellow believers (verse 8). John has learned well from the Lord Jesus Christ (see *John* 13:34–35; *Matt.* 7:15–20). Just as righteousness (1:6; 2:4–5; 3:7) and right belief (2:23; 4:2–3) are marks of the new birth, so also is love, self-denying, sacrificial service for the sake of others (see 3:16–18).

Second, *we are to love one another because 'God so loved us'* (verses 9–11). These verses encapsulate the wonder of the gospel. God's great love for us was 'made manifest' by his sending 'his only Son into the world, so that we might live through him'. God's love for us was not an empty sentiment. In order that we might have 'life', the Father sent his only begotten Son into the darkness and sin of our fallen world. God the Father gave what was most precious to

[59]

him, his only begotten Son, to secure our everlasting good (see *2 Cor.* 9:15).

The incarnation of God's Son was for a purpose, 'so that we might live through him'. He became one with us and one of us in order to rescue us from our sin and death and win for us eternal life (see *Heb.* 2:14–18). God did not spare his own Son (*Rom.* 8:32a) in his purposed desire to save us from the judgment and condemnation our sin against him deserved.

But John has not yet reached the height of God's love for us. This is seen, not in the glory of the incarnation, but in the glory of the crucifixion (verse 10). The God who 'did not spare his own Son', 'gave him up for us all' (*Rom.* 8:32). The incarnation was not an end in itself. The ultimate manifestation of God's love is not seen at Bethlehem, but at Calvary: 'In this is love, not that we have loved God but that he loved us and sent his Son to be the propitiation for our sins' (see the earlier comment on 2:2).

But here we do not have a loving Son turning aside the wrath of his angry Father. No. Here we see the God who is love sending his own and dearly loved Son to be the 'propitiation for our sins'. Nor are we to think that God's Son was a reluctant sacrifice. He said, 'I am the good shepherd...and I lay down my life for the sheep . . . No one takes it from me, but I lay it down of my own accord' (*John* 10:14–18). Remarkably, he also said, 'For this reason the Father loves me, because I lay down my life that I may take it up again' (*John* 10:17). The Father had always loved his Son, but as his Son, in obedience to his will, freely offered himself a sacrifice for our sin, the Father loved him as the Saviour of his people.

Here, then is how greatly God has loved us. Since, then, 'God so loved us, we also ought to love one another.' How can we be the recipients of such amazing love and continue to harbour grudges and resentments, and engage in petty squabbles? 'No-one who has been to the cross and seen God's immeasurable and unmerited love displayed there can go back to a life of selfishness' (Stott on *The Epistles of John*, p. 163).

John never forgets he is writing as a pastor. He understands that the supreme motivation for godly living lies in us grasping the wonder of God's love for us. The sheer undeserved kindness (grace) of God's love for us should inspire us to 'love one another'.

The antidote to dissensions and squabbles is to go back to the cross and reflect again on the self-denying, self-sacrificing love of our Lord Jesus Christ, who died 'the righteous for the unrighteous, that he might bring us to God' (*1 Pet.* 3:18). It was for sinners, for his enemies, not his friends, that he laid down his life (*Rom.* 5:8–10). Such divine love puts a sword through all our pride and self-importance, and summons us to love one another. Once again we see here the 'gospel method'. What constrains obedience to God's commands (and loving one another is a command) is 'the grace of the Lord Jesus Christ'.

Third, *we are to love one another because thereby, 'his love is perfected in us'* (verse 12). The love of the unseen God is brought to perfection 'in us'. The thought is staggering. How is our world, languishing in spiritual darkness, ever to 'see' God? 'No one has ever seen God', and yet 'if we love one another, God abides in us and his love is perfected in us'. It is Christian love that reveals the unseen God. God's love remains 'incomplete', 'imperfect', if we do not love one another. How is our fallen, sinful world ever to know what God is like? People do not read the Bible. They do not sit under the ministry of God's Word. God's purpose is that his glory will radiate from the lives and lifestyles of his people. When we love one another with Calvary love, God truly 'abides in us and his love is perfected in us'. The church is the world's window to God. What does the world around you and your church see of the glory of God? Do we radiate to the world that God is love, holy, righteous, sacrificial, life-transforming love?

17

Perfect Love

B y *this we know that we abide in him and he in us, because he has given us of his Spirit.* [14] *And we have seen and testify that the Father has sent his Son to be the Saviour of the world.* [15] *Whoever confesses that Jesus is the Son of God, God abides in him, and he in God.* [16] *So we have come to know and to believe the love that God has for us. God is love, and whoever abides in love abides in God, and God abides in him.* [17] *By this is love perfected with us, so that we may have confidence for the day of judgment, because as he is so also are we in this world.* [18] *There is no fear in love, but perfect love casts out fear. For fear has to do with punishment, and whoever fears has not been perfected in love.* [19] *We love because he first loved us.* [20] *If anyone says, 'I love God,' and hates his brother, he is a liar; for he who does not love his brother whom he has seen cannot love God whom he has not seen.* [21] *And this commandment we have from him: whoever loves God must also love his brother* (1 John 4:13–21).

The language and imagery John uses in these verses to describe what it is to be a Christian echoes, indeed employs that used by Jesus in *John* 14–17 (especially 15:1–17). It is the language of mutual indwelling: God abides in us and we abide in him (verses 13, 15, 16). Just as branches are grafted into a tree and become part of the tree and come to share its life, so Christians are joined to Christ and become sharers in his very life (*John* 15:5). So much so, that our lives are 'hidden with Christ in God' (*Col.* 3:3). The gospel does not merely bring us the forgiveness of sins, it brings us into union with God in Christ. Faith takes the believing sinner 'into Christ'. Indeed, Paul's most characteristic description of a Christian is someone who is 'in Christ' (see, for example, *Eph.* 1:1). This is true of everyone who has put his or her trust exclusively in God's Son, Jesus Christ. John is not content merely to state this truth; he proceeds in a number of ways to reassure his 'little children' that God truly does dwell in them and they in him. His great purpose in writing this letter has been to assure them that they 'have eternal life' (5:13). God wants his believing children to 'know' (verse 13) that they are his children. As a caring pastor, John knows that lack of assurance is a spiritual disease that needs to be cured. So, he proceeds to minister God's reassuring medicine for the spiritually unsure.

He first reminds them that 'we know that we abide in him and he in us because he has given us of his Spirit' (verse 13) The Holy Spirit is the risen Lord's gift to everyone who believes in him (see *Acts* 2:38; *Rom.* 8:9; *John* 16:7). Every Christian is indwelt by God's Spirit. You cannot be a Christian otherwise.

It is not immediately clear what John means here. What is the connection between God giving us 'of his Spirit' and our knowing that 'we abide in him and he in us'? There are perhaps two not un-related ways in which we may understand the connection.

John could possibly be thinking here of the 'inner witness of the Spirit', whereby he testifies to our spirits that we truly are God's children (see *Rom.* 8:15–16). This 'inner witness of the Spirit' is, however, a witness that 'bears witness *with our spirit* that we are God's children' (*Rom.* 8:16). It is a 'conjoined' witness. In other words, the Holy Spirit does not bear witness of God's adoption to lives that have no witness *in themselves* to their adoption. Rather, the Spirit, as it were, confirms to us the truth of the faltering tes-timony of our own hearts. We look at ourselves and see grace, but grace that is inconsistent, weak and punctuated by sin. The devil then begins his whispering campaign, 'How could someone like you possibly be a child of God?' But God's Spirit has a gracious ministry in our lives to confound the devil's lies.

In Paul's exposition of this great truth in *Rom.* 8:15–16, the Spirit's witness to our adoption appears to occur when we cry, 'Abba! Father!' As we face a particular crisis, the 'cry' (the same word is used of our Lord Jesus' loud cry from the cross, *Mark* 15:34) that rings from our hearts is, 'Father!' As God's children we instinctively reach out to the God who has fathered us in the gospel.

This 'witness' of the indwelling Spirit to our adoption, however, is never given to lives that do not bear the fruit of the Spirit (see *Gal.* 5:19–23). The Holy Spirit who witnesses to our spirits that we truly are God's children, is the same Holy Spirit who, from the moment of our new birth, is at work in us to conform us to the likeness of God's Son (*2 Cor.* 3:18). The assurance of our abiding in God and he in us never rests on mystical experiences, however intense or dramatic. Rather, his presence in us is confirmed by the transformation of our lives to reflect the grace and love of our Lord Jesus Christ.

The Spirit's inner witness does not mean we are never to examine ourselves to see whether we are in the faith (*2 Cor.* 13:5). But it is the gracious work of God's Spirit to assure God's children that they truly are his children, notwithstanding their sin and inconsistency. Is this not what any good father would want his children to know?

In addition to the persuading ministry of the Holy Spirit, we have the objective testimony of Christ's own apostles (verse 14). The Christian faith is no figment or fairy tale: ' . . . we have seen' (see 1:1–3; *2 Pet.* 1:16). The faith of believers rests on the impregnable rock of God's acts in history and it is the ministry of the Holy Spirit to open our eyes to recognize the truth of Christ, to desire the truth, believe the truth, and build our lives upon the truth. Our confidence as Christians rests upon what God has done in sending 'his Son to be the Saviour of the world'. The objective testimony of God's mighty acts in history is the unshakable foundation for our faith.

The Holy Spirit and the Holy Scriptures he inspired (*2 Pet.* 1:19–21) are impregnable assurances for the child of God. The Spirit of God and the revealed, written Word of God are never to be separated. When the Spirit is divorced from the Word, there is no objective standard by which we can 'test the spirits to see whether they are from God' (4:1), and no safeguard against self-induced or emotionally-induced excesses. The wisdom of *Isa.* 8:20 should always be in the forefront of our minds: 'To the teaching and to the testimony! If they will not speak according to this word, it is because they have no dawn.' If we divorce the Word from the Spirit, it is only too easy to become dryly, even deadly, orthodox.

Our words are accurate and biblical, but they have nothing of the Spirit's life and power flowing through them.

The substance of the apostles' eyewitness testimony is 'that the Father has sent his Son to be the Saviour of the world'. This is a wonderfully compact statement. It highlights Jesus' pre-existent status – he is the Son who was sent by his Father. He did not become God's Son at his incarnation. He ever was the Son and it was as the Son that he became flesh (*John* 1:14). It further highlights Jesus' status as Saviour. He is the only Saviour God has given to this world (*Acts* 4:12). Our Lord was self-consciously aware of his unqualified uniqueness as the Saviour of the world (see *John* 14:6; 8:12; 11:25).

Jesus is not one of many, or even the supreme of many. He is the only begotten of the Father, the One who was with God in the beginning and who was 'face to face with God' (*John* 1:1–3). He is not only the 'propitiation for our sins', he is also the propitiation 'for the sins of the whole world' (2:2). No matter where you go in this world, Jesus Christ is the only name 'under heaven given among men by which we must be saved' (*Acts* 4:12). It is not surprising then that God abides in those who confess 'that Jesus is the Son of God', and that they abide in him (verse 15; see 4:2; *John* 3:16, 36). The very fact that we confess that Jesus is the Son of God is evidence of this.

By nature we are children of God's wrath (*Eph.* 2:3) and blind to 'the gospel of the glory of Christ, who is the image of God' (*2 Cor.* 4:4). Left to ourselves we would never confess that Jesus is the Son of God, come in the flesh. But God comes to indwell us by his Spirit in order that we will confess Jesus as Lord and embrace him as our Saviour, and so be saved (see *Rom.* 10:9–10). By the gracious ministry of his Spirit, God implants the seed of new life within us, so that we will freely and gladly confess Jesus as Lord.

To 'confess' that Jesus is the Son of God is, of course, from one perspective the easiest of things to do. Many, perhaps, routinely confess Jesus in reciting creeds and in singing hymns, but their hearts are far from him (see *Mark* 7:6). Confessing that Jesus is the Son of God, however, means acknowledging with your mind and embracing with your heart that he is the sent One of the Father, who 'has come in the flesh' (4:2) to make atonement for our sin (2:2). Confessing Jesus means living under his lordship (see 2:3–4).

When we believingly confess that Jesus is the Son of God we 'come to know and believe the love God has for us' (verse 16). It is not, of course, that God begins to love us only when we confess his Son. Indeed, it is his prior love for us that enables us ever to believe in his Son and to confess him as Saviour and Lord. But when we confess Christ we come to know that love in our hearts.

In verse 16 John wonderfully links the themes of believing and loving. Where there is true faith that rests on Christ alone for salvation, love will and must be present, for God is love. If God does abide in us, and he is love, then his indwelling presence will betray itself in a loving lifestyle, where self-interest has been, and is being, replaced by self-sacrifice for the good of others. It is surely significant that Paul tells us, 'The fruit of the Spirit is love . . .' (*Gal.* 5:22), and Jesus tells us, 'By this all people will know that you are my disciples, if you have love for one another' (*John* 13:35).

In verses 17–21, John continues to minister the reassurance of God's grace to his 'little children'. He does so by answering a question that haunts many people: How can I have confidence before God on the day of judgment? Notice that John is absolutely certain that there will be 'the day of judgment'. As we have noted, life is not an endless cycle. History is moving inexorably towards its God-appointed goal, when Jesus Christ will return in great power and glory to 'judge the living and the dead' (see *Matt.* 25:31–46; *2 Thess.* 1:5–10).

How then, in this particular context, are we to have 'confidence for the day of judgment'? John's answer is both surprising and remarkable: 'By this is love perfected with us, so that we may have confidence for the day of judgment, because as he is so also are we in this world.' Our standing before God depends on us trusting the Lord Jesus Christ alone for salvation. But John wants us to understand that the faith that alone justifies us always manifests itself in a transformed lifestyle. This is what so exposed the lies of the false teachers who claimed to know God and were unsettling John's 'little children' (see 2:3–6). John is adamant that likeness to Jesus is the evidence that God truly indwells us and that we truly believe in his Son (*2 Cor.* 3:18).

This is what he means by love being 'perfected with us'. Perfected love is becoming like Christ, 'because as he is so also are we in this world'. John never tires of reminding us that the Christian life is a morally transformed life, patterned after the likeness of God's Son. The 'new creation' that we are becoming 'in Christ' (*2 Cor.* 5:17), is nothing less than conformity to Christ, the perfect Son. This indeed is God's ultimate purpose for believers, to conform us 'to the image of his Son, in order that he might be the firstborn among many brothers' (*Rom.* 8:29).

It is important to notice John's use of the plural, 'us', 'we'. He is thinking of God's love in the church fellowship. Love is relational. Love is not a mere sentiment; it is self-denying service for the sake of others. However much the 'antichrists' proclaimed their relationship with God, the absence of love in their lives betrayed them. When we see Christ-like love shaping the life of our churches, then we know that God himself is in us and with us – and the world also will know (see *John* 13:35).

This is why we need not 'fear' (verse 18) the day of judgment. Knowing that God loves us and knowing that we love him banishes all fears. Indeed, 'perfect love casts out fear. For fear has to do with punishment, and whoever fears has not been perfected in love'.

Being perfected in love means being assured, not so much about our love for God as about his love for us. It means grasping that the cross is the public demonstration of God's love for sinners (see 4:10). Our Lord Jesus Christ has borne in full the punishment our sin deserved:

> *Payment God cannot twice demand,*
> *First at my bleeding Surety's hand,*
> *And then again at mine.*

> Augustus Montague Toplady,
> *From whence this fear and unbelief?*

God's perfect love casts out all fear because our Saviour, as our representative Head, has stood in our place and 'suffered once for sins, the righteous for the unrighteous, that he might bring us to God' (*1 Pet.* 3:18). Christians can face every crisis in life knowing that they are loved by God and that 'neither death nor life, nor angels nor rulers, nor things present nor things to come, nor powers, nor height nor depth, nor anything else in all creation, will be able to separate us from the love of God in Christ Jesus our Lord' (*Rom.* 8:38–39).

The great truth under-girding all of this is that 'we love because he first loved us' (verse 19). Our love for God is a responsive love; it is the response of a saved sinner to a gracious, loving Saviour. The amazing thing, of course, is that God loved us when there was nothing in us worthy of his love. He loved us 'while we were still sinners' (*Rom.* 5:8). His love is wholly undeserved. It is a sovereign love, a love that will leave us exclaiming throughout eternity, 'Why, O Lord, such love to me?'

The concluding verses of the chapter are in the nature of a summary statement. John clearly has the 'antichrists' in view, those who 'went out from us, but were not of us' (2:19). They made great claims, not least that they loved God; but their claim was fraudulent. Why? Because they did not love their Christian brothers! If the language of faith ('I love God') is not matched by the life of faith ('we ought to lay down our lives for the brothers', 3:16), then our Christian profession is a lie and we are 'liars'. John highlights the sheer absurdity of claiming to love the unseen God, while hating his seen children. Indeed, in 3:23, John has told us that loving God and loving our Christian brothers is one command!

The commandment that 'we have from him' (verse 21) is possibly *Matt.* 22:37–40. There, Jesus answers the question, 'Which is the greatest commandment in the Law?' He replies, 'You shall love . . . your neighbour as yourself.' Loving one another is a command of our Lord Jesus Christ. We can be too influenced by the age we live in and conclude that Christian love is a sentiment to cultivate. First and foremost, however, it is a command to obey. We cannot cultivate a relationship with God in Christ and not, at the same time, cultivate a relationship with God's people. For the Lord Jesus Christ is inseparable from his people. He is the Head and we are his Body. He is the Bridegroom and we are his Bride. Loving one another, as we all know however, is no easy thing. We are sinners, often selfish, proud, withdrawn. There is, however, a 'key' that we are to use to help us obey this royal command. As he prepared to face the cross, Jesus gave his disciples this admonition: 'Just as I have loved you, you also are to love one another' (*John*

13:34). The starting point in loving one another is the Saviour's love for us.

As we increasingly grasp the wonder of his undeserved, gracious, sacrificial love for us, we are compelled to love one another. When we find it hard to love others, our great need is to return to the cross and be humbled again by that 'love so amazing, so divine, [that] demands my soul, my life, my all'. If we fail to love one another we make Jesus and his gospel incredible in the eyes of the world (*John* 13:35) and put a huge question mark over our Christian profession. 'Whoever loves God must also love his brother' (verse 21b).

18

Overcoming the World

*E*veryone who believes that Jesus is the Christ has been born of God, and everyone who loves the Father loves whoever has been born of him. ² By this we know that we love the children of God, when we love God and obey his commandments. ³ For this is the love of God, that we keep his commandments. And his commandments are not burdensome. ⁴ For everyone who has been born of God overcomes the world. And this is the victory that has overcome the world—our faith. ⁵ Who is it that overcomes the world except the one who believes that Jesus is the Son of God? (1 John 5:1–5).

John continues in this section to apply the reassuring medicine of God's truth to his dearly loved 'little children'. He is resolved that they shall become as certain as he is himself that they are indeed God's children. In verse 1 he returns to the foundation of all truly Christian faith, that we believe 'that Jesus is the Christ'. John is absolutely emphatic, 'Everyone who believes that Jesus is the Christ has been born of God.' The first evident sign of the new birth is that we 'believe'. Faith 'that Jesus is the Christ' is a sure sign that God's Spirit has opened our eyes to the truth concerning Jesus. The new birth opens our eyes to see that Jesus is God's long-promised Saviour.

In the Old Testament, prophets, priests, and kings were anointed with oil and set apart to lead and serve God's people. Jesus is God's final prophet (*Heb.* 1:1–2); God's ultimate priest (*Heb.* 1:3; 7:26–28; 9:24–28); and God's transcendent king (*Matt.* 28:18–20). In the new birth (see *John* 3:1–8), God implants new life in us, giving us eyes that see the truth and hearts that embrace it. This new birth is a sovereign act of God, but God principally uses his Word

to effect it in our lives (*Rom.* 10:17; *James* 1:18; *1 Pet.* 1:23). 'The
entrance of your words gives light' (*Psa.* 119:130, NKJV).

The word 'Everyone' is intended to be the greatest of encouragements and comforts to us. No matter how young, or insignificant,
or poor, or needy, if you have believed that 'Jesus is the Christ',
you have been born of God and are one of his children.

John, is careful, however, to follow his first 'everyone' with a
second 'everyone': 'and everyone who loves the Father loves whoever has been born of him'. The faith that believes that Jesus is
the Christ also loves God's children. Saving faith is not limited
to giving intellectual assent to certain truths about Jesus. Saving
faith operates through love (*Gal.* 5:6). We are justified through
faith alone, but the faith that justifies us does not exist alone. How
could it? If faith unites us to Christ, then the life of Christ will, in
some measure, become evident in our lives: it is by our fruits that
we are known to belong to God's Son (*John* 15:8). Chief among
those fruits is love for everyone who has been born of God (see
John 13:35). Again and again John shows that he has listened well
and learned well from his Saviour.

What we read here is a huge challenge to us. It is all too easy to
love those Christians who belong to our denomination or group
and who agree with us. But how are we to relate to Christians who
are different from us? The new birth unites us in God's family and,
somehow, without letting go our deeply held biblical convictions,
we must express that family unity in the way in which we think of
and treat one another. We cannot remind ourselves too often that
if we do not love our brother whom we can see, we cannot claim
meaningfully to love God whom we have not seen (4:20).

There will inevitably be differences among Christians. On
earth God washes our hearts, it is in heaven, however, that he will
thoroughly wash our heads! But our differences are 'family differences', and so we should ever 'speak the truth in love' one to the
other (*Eph.* 4:15), never forgetting that 'Christ is . . . in all' (*Col.*
3:11).

If our Father loves all of his children, and our Lord Jesus died
to save all of God's children, and the Holy Spirit indwells all of
God's children, it would be inconceivable that Christians should
not love one another. This does not mean that we do not seek to

instruct, challenge, or even rebuke one another. It does mean, however, that we do so as 'family'.

John returns in verse 2 to the question: What does it mean to love God's children? (see 3:11–18). How can we 'know' that we truly love our fellow believers? John does not leave us in doubt: 'By this we know that we love the children of God, when we love God and obey his commandments' (verse 2). Just what is the connection between loving God, keeping his commandments and loving his children? We love God's children when we relate to them in a life shaped and fashioned by love to God and obedience to his commandments.

Love to God is expressed in a glad, evangelical keeping of his commandments (see *John* 14:15, 21, 23). One of those commandments is, 'Love your neighbour as yourself' (indeed, this is a summary of the second table of the Law: see *Matt.* 22:34–40, especially verse 39). Failure to love our neighbour as ourselves is ultimately a failure to love God and keep his commandments. This is true in family life. My wife loves me better because she loves God first. The best I can do for my wife is to ensure that I love and honour the Lord before everything else in life. All our failures in love are the result of failing to love the Lord first and best.

Throughout these verses John beautifully links together love and law. Love and law are not enemies; they are spiritual twins. Obedience to God's commandments is the way in which we express our love to him (verse 3). Most probably, John has the 'antichrists' in his sights. They lived lawless lives (see 1:6; 2:3–6). But God's true children live lawful lives, lives shaped by loving obedience to his commandments. Your attitude to God's commandments will speak volumes about the reality or unreality of your Christian profession.

Far from being weights to hold us down, 'his commandments are not burdensome' (verse 3). It is possible that John is thinking here of Jesus' words in *Matt.* 11:30, 'My yoke is easy, and my burden is light.' God's commands are no more burdensome to a Christian that wings are burdensome to a bird: 'They are the means by which we live in freedom and fulfilment' (David Jackman, *The Message of John's Letters*, Inter-Varsity Press, 1988, p. 141). His commands are good, all of them (*Psa.* 19:7–11). How could 'his' commands be burdensome? He is the God who 'did not spare his own Son but gave him up for us all [and] . . . who will also with him graciously give us all things'.

John proceeds to give us a particular reason why God's commandments are not burdensome (verse 4): 'For everyone who has been born of God overcomes the world.' There is a definite sequence of thought in the argument here. Everyone who has been born of God overcomes the world. But how is this overcoming triumph achieved? Through our faith! Faith is the victory that *has overcome* the world for the believer. The tense John uses here (an aorist) expresses a once-for-all action or event. As you put your trust in the once-for-all, finished work of Christ, you become a sharer in his triumph over sin and death and hell. Faith takes you on to the victory side where Jesus reigns (*John* 16:33 – Jesus has overcome the world).

In this way the world (see 2:15–17) and its seductive hold has been forever broken in the believer's life. God's commands are now preferred above and before everything the world has to offer, and they are seen, in the light of the cross, for what they truly are, the commands of a loving, merciful Father who desires and pursues our best. Faith sees with new eyes the grace and wisdom of God's law (see *Rom.* 3:31).

In verse 5, John uses a present tense to describe the Christian's relationship to the world. The Christian 'has overcome' the world, but he also 'overcomes' the world. We share in the once-for-all triumph of our Saviour, but we are called to make that once-for-all triumph a daily reality in our lives through believing 'that Jesus is the Son of God', that the incarnate Jesus is God's eternal Son (verse 5).

The old illustration of slaves being emancipated during the American Civil War (1861–5) makes the point well. They had been freed, but many continued to live like slaves. Their great need was to realize in their lives the truth of their emancipation. So it is with the Christian. Through the power of the gospel we have been 'set free from sin, [and] have become slaves of righteousness' (*Rom.* 6:18). In Christ, by faith, we have overcome the world, and by that same faith in Christ we daily overcome the world when we refuse its seductions and temptations and live to please our great

Overcomer, Jesus Christ. Faith is not a static grace. Every day we are to apply the living grace of faith in Christ to the 'pull' of this fallen, Christ-denying, God-rejecting world. It is our faith in the Lord Jesus Christ that 'connects' us to the resources of his triumph.

19

Believing God's Testimony

*T*his is he who came by water and blood—Jesus Christ; not by the water only but by the water and the blood. And the Spirit is the one who testifies, because the Spirit is the truth. [7] For there are three that testify: [8] the Spirit and the water and the blood; and these three agree. [9] If we receive the testimony of men, the testimony of God is greater, for this is the testimony of God that he has borne concerning his Son. [10] Whoever believes in the Son of God has the testimony in himself. Whoever does not believe God has made him a liar, because he has not believed in the testimony that God has borne concerning his Son. [11] And this is the testimony, that God gave us eternal life, and this life is in his Son. [12] Whoever has the Son has life; whoever does not have the Son of God does not have life (1 John 5:6–12).

L ying behind much of what John writes is the dark spectre of the 'antichrists' and the 'many false prophets' who were unsettling John's readers with their teaching. Understanding what these 'liars' taught will help us grasp what John is telling us in these verses. He has written 'that Jesus is the Son of God' (5:5). Now he tells us, 'This is he who came by water and blood' (5:6). Eight times in this section John uses the words 'testifies', 'testify', and 'testimony'. It is as if we are in a courtroom and John is bringing forward witnesses to testify on Jesus' behalf, that he is the Christ, the Son of God. John highlights three witnesses in particular, the Spirit, the water, and the blood (verses 6–8). John possibly also has in mind *Deut.* 19:15, 'Only on the evidence of two witnesses or of three witnesses shall a charge be established.' God has supplied infallible witnesses to testify to his truth.

We first need to ask what John means by 'the water and the blood'. In his Gospel, John bore personal testimony to 'blood and water' coming out of Jesus' spear-pierced side (*John* 19:34–35). It is possible that here 'the water and the blood' (not 'blood and water' as in *John* 19:34) signifies the incontestable fact of Jesus' death on the cross. God's Christ, his own Son, actually died. The One who 'came', came by 'water and blood'.

It seems more likely, however, that John is thinking of the water of Jesus' baptism. For one thing, the water and the blood are separate witnesses ('For there are three that testify: the Spirit and the water and the blood', verses 7–8). Secondly, John is clear that he did 'not come by water only but by *the* water and *the* blood' (notice the two definite articles).

John is probably indicating that there were those who taught that Jesus came by the water only. The false teachers who were unsettling John's readers appear to have taught that it was inconceivable that God's Christ could die. Death was the ultimate sign of weakness. These 'antichrists' were doing what heretics in every age do – rationalizing the gospel, configuring it to what they thought appropriate and acceptable. Here John is confronting their denial that Jesus Christ died. The heretics accepted that Jesus Christ 'came by water', that he was baptized. They denied, however, that he also came by 'blood'; that God's Christ would or even could die. John is adamant, 'This is he who came by water and blood – Jesus Christ; not by the water only but by the water and the blood' (verse 6).

John's concern here is not simply to affirm the historical facts concerning Jesus. If it was not God's own Son (verse 5), his Christ, who died on the cross, there is no salvation. The significance of the cross lies in who it was who died there. No mere man, however favoured of God, could make effective atonement for sin and restore lost sinners to peace and fellowship with God.

Thus there is the witness of 'the water and the blood' (verses 6 and 8). Jesus 'came by water and blood' (verse 6). At his baptism, the Spirit of God came upon Jesus (anointing him publicly for his mission), and a 'voice from heaven said, "This is my beloved Son, with whom I am well pleased"' (*Matt.* 3:17). The same Jesus who 'came' by water also 'came' by blood. It was Jesus Christ, the Son of God, who died on the cross. As much as his baptism, Jesus' death on the cross was a public fact. The Spirit who came upon

Jesus at his baptism, publicly anointing him for his saving mission, upheld and supported him on his cross. To the truth of these great facts the Spirit testifies. He is the divine Persuader, sealing the truth of Christ to our hearts and minds.

There is little doubt that John is thinking here about the 'internal testimony or witness of the Spirit'. Alongside the objective facts of the gospel, there is the unseen but powerful ministry of the Holy Spirit who 'testifies' (present tense) to the saving truth of Christ. He opens our eyes to acknowledge the truth, inclines our wills to embrace the truth, and stirs our hearts to love the truth. It is the Spirit's ministry to make the facts of Christ 'come to life' before our eyes and in our hearts.

John Owen, the great English Puritan, often distinguished between knowing the truth and knowing the power of the truth. It is the Holy Spirit's ministry to seal the truth of God's Son to our hearts so that we experience its power. 'He it is', says John Calvin, 'who seals in our hearts the testimony of the water and the blood.' The Holy Spirit is the Spirit of truth (see *John* 14:17; 16:13) and it is the truth of Jesus' divine-human identity and his saving work that he seals authoritatively to our minds and hearts. The Holy Spirit, then, is the key witness; and his testimony is incontrovertible, because it is the testimony of God (verse 9). God cannot lie.

John highlights here the supernatural character of the Christian faith. The gospel is more than acknowledging or confessing certain facts about Jesus, however orthodox and evangelical. It is God the Holy Spirit's ministry to work inwardly in our lives, opening the eyes of our understanding, inclining our wills and persuading our hearts to receive and rest upon Christ alone for pardon and acceptance with God. *The Larger Catechism* of the Westminster Assembly memorably highlights this. To the question, 'What is justifying faith?' (Q. 72), the answer is given: 'Justifying faith is a saving grace, wrought in the heart of a sinner by the Spirit and word of God, whereby he, being convinced of his sin and misery, and of the disability in himself and all other creatures to recover him out of his lost condition, not only assenteth to the truth of the promise of the gospel, but receiveth and resteth upon Christ and his righteousness, therein held forth, for pardon of sin, and for the accepting and accounting of his person righteous in the sight of God for salvation.' The 'natural person', the man without the Spirit, 'does not accept the things of the Spirit of God, for they are folly to him, and he is not able to understand them because they are spiritually discerned' (*1 Cor.* 2:14). We need God's Spirit to dispel the spiritual darkness from our minds and hearts and to illuminate our lives with the 'light of the knowledge of the glory of God in the face of Jesus Christ' (*2 Cor.* 4:6). When the Holy Spirit does illuminate our lives in this way, his testimony is inwardly persuasive (verse 10).

Against the lies of the false teachers and antichrists, John assures his beloved that 'Whoever believes in the Son of God has the testimony in himself.' Our faith in the incarnate, crucified and risen Son of God is confirmed by the inward testimony of the Spirit. When people refuse to 'believe God', that is to believe the truth of his testimony concerning his Son, they make him out to be a liar (verse 10b). The apostles' witness to the Lord Jesus Christ was the witness of eyewitnesses (see 1:1–3; *2 Pet.* 1:16). Even more, it was the witness of men who spoke from God 'as they were carried along by the Holy Spirit' (*2 Pet.* 1:21). This is exactly what Jesus said they would do as his witnesses (see *John* 16:13). A refusal to believe this God-inspired testimony makes God out to be a liar. In receiving the Bible as the Word of God, we are receiving and believing God's testimony concerning his own Son. The apostles' testimony is the testimony of God himself.

The issue, however, is not simply that in refusing God's testimony we make him out to be a liar. The result of this refusal has eternal ramifications. When God sent his Son into the world, he sent him to secure for lost sinners 'eternal life'. Eternal life is not so much life that is endless, as life that is lived in unending fellowship with the God who is life (see *John* 17:3; 14:6).

Jesus Christ is life, true life, the life that restores us to fellowship with God. To have the Son is to have 'life', salvation from eternal death and unending communion with God. In contrast, 'whoever does not have the Son of God does not have life'. The life every human heart aches for is found in union with the Son of God, Jesus Christ (see 5:20b). It is the most serious of all matters to refuse to accept God's testimony concerning his Son. God's incarnate, crucified and risen Son is 'the way, the truth and the life', and no one comes to the Father except by him (*John* 14:6). For the New Testament, salvation, eternal life, is not a doctrine to believe, abstracted from a Person to receive. Jesus Christ himself is the believer's salvation.

20

Assurance before God

I write these things to you who believe in the name of the Son of God that you may know that you have eternal life. [14] And this is the confidence that we have toward him, that if we ask anything according to his will he hears us. [15] And if we know that he hears us in whatever we ask, we know that we have the requests that we have asked of him. [16] If anyone sees his brother committing a sin not leading to death, he shall ask, and God will give him life—to those who commit sins that do not lead to death. There is sin that leads to death; I do not say that one should pray for that. [17] All wrongdoing is sin, but there is sin that does not lead to death. [18] We know that everyone who has been born of God does not keep on sinning, but he who was born of God protects him, and the evil one does not touch him. [19] We know that we are from God, and the whole world lies in the power of the evil one. [20] And we know that the Son of God has come and has given us understanding, so that we may know him who is true; and we are in him who is true, in his Son Jesus Christ. He is the true God and eternal life. [21] Little children, keep yourselves from idols (1 John 5:13–21).

John now highlights the particular reason why he wrote this letter: 'that you may know that you have eternal life'. He is writing to Christians, to those who 'believe in the name of the Son of God', who had been unsettled in their faith by the teaching of the 'many false prophets' (4:1). It is probable, as we have seen, that these 'false prophets' were the 'many antichrists' who had once been part of the Christian church (2:18–19). As a caring pastor, John wrote to assure them that 'eternal life', unending fellowship with God, is the possession of everyone ('whoever' in verse 12) who believes 'in the name of the Son of God'.

Salvation in found in Christ alone. It is also true that everyone who believes in the name of the Son of God lives a new life. This new life is seen in a new commitment to keeping God's commandments (2:3–6; 3:10; see also 1:5–10) and in a new commitment to loving the brothers see 3:14; 4:20. Where these 'marks of grace' are absent from our lives we can hardly claim to have been born of God (see 2:29; 4;7).

Christian assurance is therefore double-edged. God graciously gives us the inner witness of the Holy Spirit (verse 10), who seals to our hearts the truth of our adoption. But the Holy Spirit never seals assurance of salvation to anyone who is not keeping God's commandments and loving the brothers.

These closing verses breathe assurance. Five times John writes 'we know' (verses 15, 18, 19, 20). This is not arrogant presumption, but rather the humble assurance of a child who knows his Father. Indeed, in verse 20, John traces all Christian assurance to its true source, Christ himself: 'The Son of God . . . has given us understanding.'

In *verses 14–17*, John highlights a vital area of the Christian life where the believer has unbounded confidence ('boldness'). So sure are the children of God of their relationship to God that, 'if we ask anything according to his will he hears us. And if we know that he hears us in whatever we ask, we know that we have the requests that we have asked of him' (verses 14 and 15). At the heart of true prayer is a relationship (think, for example, of 'Our Father in heaven . . . '). Jesus laboured to teach his own disciples the nature of true prayer see *Matt.* 6:5–15; 7:7–11. In prayer, as the children of God we bring our heart's desires to the heavenly Father, in Jesus' name. Our Father, who loves all his children, has promised not only to hear but also to answer all our prayers. It is because he loves us that he only answers our prayers 'according to his will' (see *Matt.* 7:11).

The great exemplar of believing prayer is our Lord Jesus Christ. As he faced the prospect of the cross, he cried out to his Father, 'If it is possible, let this cup pass from me, nevertheless, not as I will, but as you will' (*Matt.* 26:39). Three times, Matthew tells us, he prayed the same prayer (*Matt.* 26:44), each time concluding his anguished prayer, 'not as I will, but as you will'. Every truly

Christian prayer has this same spoken or unspoken conclusion. God graciously shuts his ears, as it were, to requests for what will be neither for our truest good, nor for his glory. In prayer the Christian expresses confidence in such a God.

In verses 16 and 17, John illustrates the confidence the Christian has in prayer, and its limits. While the particulars in these two verses are difficult to be completely certain about, the general thrust of their teaching is clear. We see a 'brother committing a sin not leading to death'. What are we to do? We are to 'ask', that is ask God, and he 'will give him life'. This is surely a wonderful encouragement for Christians to pray. Our Father does not want any of his children to fall into sin and make shipwreck of their lives. His will is that all his children should be recovered, and prayer is one of the principal means he uses to restore them. Pastoral care in the church is not the exclusive responsibility of the pastors and elders (see *Gal.* 6:1). Every Christian is compelled by the obligation of love to seek the spiritual good of his fellow Christians. We are our brother's keeper (see *Gen.* 4:9). As John Bunyan quaintly put it, 'We can do more than pray after we have prayed, but we cannot do more than pray until we have prayed.'

So much is clear. But what is *the sin that does not lead to death* and what is *the sin that does lead to death*? (verse 16). John is clear that 'All wrongdoing is sin' (verse 17). The Bible is no less clear that 'the wages of sin is death' (*Rom.* 6:23). And yet, John distinguishes here between the sin that does not lead to death and the sin that does lead to death. What does he mean?

The context of John's words is all-important. The sin that leads to death appears to be the sin that marked out the antichrists, the sin that denies that Jesus is God's incarnate Son and that salvation is found alone in him (see 4:2–3). By denying that Jesus came 'in the flesh' (4:2) and that he died a sin-bearing death, the antichrists cut themselves off from the One who is the only propitiation for 'the sins of the whole world' (see the note on 2:2). In contrast, the sin that does not lead to death is sin that does not deny that Jesus is the Christ, the Son of God in our flesh, the divinely-provided 'propitiation for our sins' (see 4:2–3; 5:1).

The death that sin deserves and that God will execute on it will only ever be avoided through believing in Christ and receiving the propitiation he has provided for us. By denying the truth concerning God's Son the antichrists consigned themselves to death, unending separation from God. They did not 'have the Son of God', and so did 'not have life' (5:12). A refusal to believe the testimony of God concerning his Son, revealed in his Word, leaves us facing a lost, unimaginable, God-less eternity. The sin that leads to death does so because it refuses to appropriate the gracious propitiation God has provided for sin in his Son.

It may be that John has in mind here Jesus' teaching on the unforgivable sin (*Luke* 12;10; *Mark* 3:29; *Matt.* 12:31–32). This sin, interestingly, is described as blasphemy 'against the Holy Spirit', who, in John's words, is the One who divinely bears witness to Jesus Christ (see 5:6–10).

John does not actually say that we should *not* pray for such people. He is saying that we can have no confidence, no assurance that God will hear our prayers for such people and give us what we ask. The Bible solemnly warns us about people like these antichrists who fall away, 'crucifying once again the Son of God to their own harm and holding him up to contempt'. 'It is impossible', says the letter to the Hebrews, 'to restore [them] again to repentance' (*Heb.* 6:4–6).

In *verses 18–21*, John concludes his letter with three categorical statements, all highlighting the assurance that is native to 'the normal Christian life'.

First, *'We know that everyone who has been born of God does not keep on sinning'* (verse 18). John picks up the language he used in 3:6, 9. At a first reading, his words seem impossible: Literally they read, 'Everyone who has been born of God does not sin.' John, of course, does not mean that Christians do not sin – we do, often, and to our shame (see 1:8–10; 2:2). How then are we to understand these words? It is possible John is saying that Christians, because they have been 'born of God', and have God's seed in them (3:9), no longer 'keep on sinning' (they do 'not continue to sin', NIV). Sin is now, because of the new birth, no longer the prevailing pattern in the Christian's life. We still sin, but not as we did before. Sin is now intermittent where it once dominated our lives. This would make sense.

It is more likely, however, that John is thinking of the 'definitive sanctification' that takes place when someone is born of God's Spirit. 'We know' this to be true, John is saying, because we understand what it means to be born of God. Through the new birth and the believer's union with Christ, sin's guilt has been removed and its power irreversibly broken. Sanctification is a progressive reality, as we are conformed, degree by degree, to the likeness of our Lord Jesus Christ (*2 Cor.* 3:18). But this progressive sanctification is the fruit, or evidence, of the definitive or decisive sanctification that takes place when the believer is 'delivered . . . from the domain of darkness and transferred . . . to the kingdom of [God's] beloved Son' (*Col.* 1:13). Paul can therefore write to the Corinthians as 'those sanctified in Christ Jesus' (*1 Cor.* 1:2). This decisive breach with sin, and its master the devil, is absolutely assured because 'he who was born of God protects [us], and the evil one does not touch [us]' (verse 18) .

Our Lord Jesus Christ keeps us safe. He is the assurance that we shall not fall away and be lost. Because it is Christ himself who protects us, 'the evil one' cannot touch us. John again reminds us of the great enemy who unceasingly seeks our downfall. He is malignant and unwearied in his attempts to harm God's children. He is a real and powerful enemy, but our Lord Jesus Christ has decisively defeated him (see 3:8; *Col.* 2:15; *Luke* 10:18). No one, certainly not the evil one, can snatch us out of Christ's hands (*John* 10:28–29).

'Does not touch [us]' does not quite convey the strength of the word John uses. He uses the word on only one other occasion (*John* 20:17), and there it clearly has the idea of 'grasping hold of'. The evil one will trouble us until the moment we die, just as he never let up seeking to trouble the Saviour. But he will not grasp hold of us; we are safe because 'the one born of God' protects us. We truly are 'more than conquerors through him who loved us' (*Rom.* 8:37).

Second, *'We know that we are from God, and the whole world lies in the power of the evil one'* (verse 19). The world we live in is divided into two camps, those who 'are from God' and those who lie 'in the power of the evil one'. To be 'from God' (literally, 'of God') is to be born of God, to be a child of God, to be indwelt by the Spirit of God (see 3:1; 4:13). Everyone who is 'of God' 'believes that Jesus is the Christ' (5:1). In contrast, 'the whole world lies in the power of the evil one'. John clearly means that this present world in its rebellion against God is under the power and dominion of Satan, the prince of darkness, the accuser of the brothers. John is in no doubt about the reality of 'the evil one'.

Satan is no figment of the religious imagination. From *Gen.* 3 Satan's presence and activity are set before us in the Bible. He is a defeated enemy (see *Gen.* 3:15; *Col.* 2:15), but remains, until Christ's coming, a powerful enemy. Peter describes him as 'a roaring lion' (*1 Pet.* 5:8), and our Lord Jesus Christ warned his disciples to 'watch and pray' constantly lest they be overtaken by Satan's temptations. The fundamental mark of Satan's power in this world is the spiritual blindness that dominates the world. It is only because God 'has shone in our hearts to give the light of the knowledge of the glory of God in the face of Jesus Christ' (*2 Cor.* 4:4, 6), that we are not still captives under Satan's rule.

Third, *'And we know that the Son of God has come . . . '* (verse 20). John links together the historical and the experiential aspects of Christian faith. Truly Christian faith, the faith that brings us into saving union with Christ, is anchored in the great fact of Christ's coming. God's Son appeared on earth (see *1 Tim.* 3:16; *John* 1:14). But saving faith is, as we have already seen, more than assenting to historical facts. So, John tells us, the Son of God who 'has come', 'has given us understanding, so that we may know him who is true'. This 'understanding' is not the result of the application of our intellects; it is the product of divine illumination – 'the Son of God . . . has given us understanding'. By nature our minds have been darkened by sin and Satan. But in his great mercy, God opens our eyes to the truth of his Son. He enables us to 'make sense' of the gospel, to understand both our great need of a Saviour and the fitness of Jesus Christ to be our Saviour. In particular, our God-given spiritual understanding enables us to 'know him who is true'. The word John uses here has more the idea of 'real' than 'true' (though perhaps *'truly real'* may be a good translation). He uses the same word in his Gospel where Jesus speaks of himself as the 'true [real] bread' (*John* 6:32) and as 'the true [real] vine' (*John* 15:10).

John has now come almost full circle. In 1:3, he wrote that the purpose of the gospel was to bring us into fellowship 'with the Father and with his Son Jesus Christ'. This is what it means to 'know him who is truly real'. The heart of spiritual knowledge is fellowship. John characteristically highlights this spiritual intimacy when he continues, 'and we are in him who is true [real], in his Son Jesus Christ'. John wants his readers to grasp the summit of their gospel blessings. Not only do they 'know him who is true', they are 'in him who is true'.

Here are the twin realities that lie at the very heart of the Christian life: *union* with God in Christ and *communion* with God in Christ. 'He is the true [real] God and eternal life'. 'He' is rather 'This'; that is, 'This is the true God.' The natural grammatical sense would link 'This' with what immediately precedes it, 'his Son Jesus Christ'. If so, then John is making an unambiguous declaration of Christ's deity. It seems a little more likely, however, not least in the light of *John* 17:3, that 'This' refers to the Father, who is clearly the subject of the two previous references to 'true' in verse 20. The possible link with *John* 17:3 ('And this is eternal life, that they know you the only true God, and Jesus Christ whom you have sent'), reminds us that 'eternal life' is fundamentally qualitative. Knowing the only true God is to possess eternal life.

John's final words are strikingly appropriate. He reminds his 'little children' of the ever-present danger of 'idols'. No matter how blessed and privileged a believer is, he must resolutely and constantly resist and refuse the temptation to embrace idols. No believer is immune from the seductive pull of the evil one and the idols he regularly brings before us. However much the child of God is comforted by the knowledge that 'he who was born of God protects him' (verse 18), he must no less recognize his responsibility to protect himself.

'Idols' are anything and anyone that would replace the Lord God as the chief delight of our hearts. The first commandment (*Exod.* 20:3), set as it is in the context of God's redeeming grace to his people (*Exod.* 20:1–2), stands sentinel over the life of the believer. How can we then best keep ourselves from idols? By following the pattern marked out in *Exod.* 20:1–3. As we reflect on God's great grace to us in his Son, we make Joseph's question our own: 'How can I do this great wickedness and sin against God?' (*Gen.* 39:9). Nothing better keeps the child of God from idols than an ever-deepening grasp of the love of God in Jesus Christ. Embracing idols in any form would then be, not only utter disloyalty, but to sin against the costly love of God, who 'did not spare his own Son but gave him up for us all' (*Rom.* 8:32). The only life worthy of the Lord who loved us and gave his own Son to rescue us from a lost, God-less eternity, is a life wholly devoted to him. More than anything else, it is the cross of our Lord Jesus Christ that compels us 'to present [our] bodies as a living sacrifice, holy and acceptable to God, which is [our] spiritual worship' (*Rom.* 12:1).

2 JOHN

*T*he elder to the elect lady and her children, whom I love in truth, and not only I, but also all who know the truth, ² because of the truth that abides in us and will be with us forever: ³ Grace, mercy, and peace will be with us, from God the Father and from Jesus Christ the Father's Son, in truth and love. ⁴ I rejoiced greatly to find some of your children walking in the truth, just as we were commanded by the Father. ⁵ And now I ask you, dear lady—not as though I were writing you a new commandment, but the one we have had from the beginning—that we love one another. ⁶ And this is love, that we walk according to his commandments; this is the commandment, just as you have heard from the beginning, so that you should walk in it. ⁷ For many deceivers have gone out into the world, those who do not confess the coming of Jesus Christ in the flesh. Such a one is the deceiver and the antichrist. ⁸ Watch yourselves, so that you may not lose what we have worked for, but may win a full reward. ⁹ Everyone who goes on ahead and does not abide in the teaching of Christ, does not have God. Whoever abides in the teaching has both the Father and the Son. ¹⁰ If anyone comes to you and does not bring this teaching, do not receive him into your house or give him any greeting, ¹¹ for whoever greets him takes part in his wicked works.¹² Though I have much to write to you, I would rather not use paper and ink. Instead I hope to come to you and talk face to face, so that our joy may be complete. ¹³ The children of your elect sister greet you (2 John).

The style, language and concerns of this Letter are very similar to those of 1 John, and it was almost certainly penned by the same author. As was 1 John, this brief Letter is concerned about false teachers. John calls them in verse 7 'deceivers' and 'the antichrist' (see *1 John* 2:18, 26). They had once belonged to God's church, but had 'gone out into the world' (verse 7; see *1 John* 2:19). These 'deceivers' also denied 'the coming of Jesus Christ in the flesh' (verse 7; see *1 John* 4:2). Against an almost identical background, then, to *1 John*, this letter was written to warn 'the elect lady and her children' 'not to lose what we have worked for' (verse 8) through being taken in by the deceivers.

John writes to 'the elect lady and her children' and sends concluding greetings from 'the children of your elect sister' (verse 13). While it is possible that John is writing to a particular Christian woman and her children, it is much more likely that these titles are personifications of local congregations. For one thing, it would be strange, not to say indelicate, for John to write to a woman and tell her that God has commanded him and the woman to 'love one another' (verse 5). In the second place, the concluding greeting, 'The children of your elect sister greet you', would make more sense if understood of a particular congregation. Thirdly, John's great concern that the 'elect lady and her children' would not be deceived by false teachers ('deceivers', verse 7), has a congregational rather than a personal feel about it.

John's purpose in writing to this particular church was to warn it to be on its guard against doctrinally aberrant infiltrators (verse 10). For him the only basis for meaningful fellowship is sound, healthy doctrine. Such a concern for sound, orthodox doctrine does not sit easily with this present age of multi-faith worship and doctrine-less ecumenism.

In this respect, however, John is simply reflecting the uniform teaching of the whole Bible. He is not being theologically narrow-minded, but pastorally sensitive. Doctrine matters. Christian unity and fellowship that is not founded upon the great doctrines of the gospel is a charade. In the professing church today we regularly hear men and women denying the doctrines of the pre-existence of Christ, the incarnation, the virgin birth, Christ's penal substitutionary atonement, his bodily resurrection and much else. For John the apostle, such men and women would be classified as deceivers and antichrists (verse 7) and would be given no opportunity to infect Christ's church with their deceptions (verses 10–11).

I

Warmest Greetings

*T*he elder to the elect lady and her children, whom I love in truth,
and not only I, but also all who know the truth, ² because of the
truth that abides in us and will be with us forever (2 John 1–2).

U nlike the First Letter, 2 John begins with a personal greeting.
John describes himself as 'the elder'. It is probable that John
is referring, not to his age but to his office in Christ's church. He is
an apostle of Christ, but he is also an elder, an overseer (*Acts* 20:17,
28; *1 Tim.* 3:1). Peter similarly describes himself as 'a fellow elder'
when he exhorted the elders of the churches to which he wrote
(*1 Pet.* 5:1). In calling himself 'the' elder, John assumes that the
church will know who is writing to them.

If we are right in thinking that 'the elect lady and her children' is
a particular Christian congregation, it is impossible to know where
this congregation was. Perhaps the general, unspecified designation
makes what he writes all the more immediately applicable to all
Christian congregations.

John assures the church that he loves them 'in truth' (there is no
'the' before 'truth'). The fact that the following two references to
'truth' are each preceded by the definite article, makes it possible
that here also John means 'the truth'; that is, that his love for them
is in accord with God's revealed truth concerning his Son, Jesus
Christ.

It is more likely however, that John is assuring his readers that
his love for them, unlike the 'love' of the false teachers, is sincere
and genuine. John's emphatic 'I' underlines the point, as if to say,
'Unlike these deceivers, who are seeking to infiltrate your gather-
ings [see verse 10], I truly love you.'

John's love, however, is not only sincere and genuine, it is in accord with 'the truth', the deposit of truth which God has revealed through his Son (see *2 Tim.* 1:13–14; *Jude* 3). Indeed, John assures his readers that 'all who know the truth' love them. To 'know' in this sense is not simply to know what the truth says, but to experience the truth, to be mastered and shaped by it. The basis of truly Christian love, then, is the unchanging truth of God. What unites Christian believers in mutual love is that we have been 'brought forth by the word of truth' (*James* 1:18).

Christians are to love their neighbours and even their enemies (*Luke* 10:25–37; *Matt.* 5:43–48). But the 'household of faith' has a special claim upon our love (see *1 Pet.* 2:17; *Gal.* 6:10). The 'truth that abides in us and will be with us forever' is our common heritage and the source of our common salvation. It 'abides in us and will be with us forever' because Jesus Christ himself is the truth and he indwells us by his Spirit in an indissoluble union of grace.

2

God's Blessing

*Grace, mercy, and peace will be with us, from God the Father
and from Jesus Christ the Father's Son, in truth and love*
(2 John 3).

John's salutation occurs, in similar words, in all of Paul's letters. 'Grace' is undeserved kindness to judgment-deserving sinners, God giving us what we could never deserve, his own Son. 'Mercy' stands in contrast with what our sins positively deserve, God's righteous wrath and judgment. 'Peace' is more than merely the absence of hostility. God's peace, his 'shalom', speaks of his pledged commitment to make us whole, to restore us and reconcile us to himself, overcoming every obstacle to secure our everlasting blessedness. 'Peace' is salvation in its fullest expression. In other words, John is not praying that these rich blessings will be with them; rather, he is assuring his readers that they will certainly be with them.

These blessings 'will be with us, from God the Father and from Jesus Christ, the Father's Son'. The fact that this triad of divine blessings is equally from the Father and the Father's Son, further highlights the pre-existent, divine sonship of Jesus Christ. This truth is both central and precious to the apostle John; see *John* 1:1, 14; 3:16.

John further tells us that these blessings will be ours 'in truth and love'. It is difficult to be clear as to what John means. This somewhat unusual expression could mean that God's 'grace, mercy and peace' will be ours only if we remain in the truth and practise love. It is also possible that John is telling us that these rich blessings come to us by the means of God's truth and love. Or

– and this would tie in with the way John uses these two words in verse 1 – 'grace, mercy and peace' may be seen as blessings that God *truly* and *lovingly* bestows upon his people.

On balance this last understanding fits the context best. Every blessing we enjoy from God is the fruit of his love to us in Christ. It is imperative that we never imagine that the Father's Son came to secure the Father's love for us. He is himself the gift and supreme evidence of the Father's love for us, a love that is as undeserved as it is glorious.

3

Walking in Truth and Love

*I rejoiced greatly to find some of your children walking in the truth,
just as we were commanded by the Father. ⁵ And now I ask you,
dear lady — not as though I were writing you a new commandment,
but the one we have had from the beginning — that we love one
another. ⁶ And this is love, that we walk according to his commandments; this is the commandment, just as you have heard from the
beginning, so that you should walk in it* (2 John 4–6).

John will soon highlight his concern about the danger he
sees this church to be in. Verse 8 crystallizes this concern:
'Watch yourselves . . .' He had learned well from his Saviour
the importance of being spiritually vigilant (see *Matt.* 26:41; *1 Pet.*
5:8). His concern for their spiritual good prompts him to warn
them and exhort them to take action against the 'many deceivers'
who threaten them (see *1 John* 4:1).

He begins, however, on a positive note: 'I rejoiced greatly to find
some of your children walking in the truth, just as we were commanded by the Father.' Although 'truth' has no definite article,
it seems clear that here John is thinking about the faith, the body
of revealed truth concerning God's Son. In the parallel verse in
3 John 4 John uses the definite article. To 'walk' in truth is to live
under the authority of the truth. God's truth is not only to be
believed and confessed, it is to be obeyed. Truth is for living!

John's rejoicing, nevertheless, is somewhat tempered. Sadly, not
all in the church were 'walking in the truth', that is, holding fast to
the 'pattern of sound words' (*2 Tim.* 1:13) and obeying God's commandments (see *1 John* 2:3–6). 'Some' were walking in the truth,
but not all. However godly and faithful a church is, it remains on

this side of glory a 'mixed multitude'. We live in the age of the 'not yet'. Only when Christ returns and his people are all transformed into his likeness (see *1 John* 3:2) will all unbelievers finally be excluded from the company of his people.

It is difficult to know whether John is thinking about a specific commandment of the Father when he says, 'as we were commanded by the Father'. It is perhaps more likely that he is thinking of the general teaching of God's Word that summons us to be doers as well as hearers of the Word (see *James* 1:22; *Matt.* 7:21–27). It is striking that the Bible appears relatively unconcerned about how someone comes to faith, but is deeply concerned that we truly believe in the Lord Jesus Christ and show in our lives the faith, obedience and love that mark us out as those who have truly come to believe in him. Professed faith that does not manifest itself in good works betrays itself as self-deceived and false (see *James* 2:14–17, *Eph.* 2:9–10).

In verse 5, John echoes words from his First Letter (2:7). The command 'that we love one another' is not something that originated with John; it was a command 'we have had from the beginning'. Most probably John is thinking about the words of the Lord Jesus he recorded in his Gospel, 13:34–35. More than anything else, self-denying love, Christ-like love, for the Christian family, is to mark us out in the world as Christ's own disciples. John includes himself in this injunction.

John's continual, even repetitive emphasis on the necessity of self-denyingly loving our fellow Christian brothers and sisters, highlights how pre-eminent this was in John's understanding of what it is to be a Christian. He would have echoed Paul's stinging words in *1 Cor.* 13: 'If I speak in the tongues of men and of angels, but have not love . . . I am nothing.'

As we have seen, and as we see in this Letter (verses 10–11), John is not advocating a love that is sentimental and lacks spiritual discernment. But whenever we encounter believers who confess and embrace the doctrines of Christ in the gospel, we are to love them as 'family' (see *1 John* 5:1).

Neither is John advocating a love that is devoid of moral content: 'And this is love, that we walk according to his commandments.' Again, John is clearly thinking of Jesus' words in *John* 14:15, 21.

Christian love is shaped and fashioned by the moral commands of Christ. Far from love and law being opposed to one another, they belong together and inform and protect one another. Love without law would lead to self-indulgence (see *Gal.* 5:13–14). Law without love would lead to cold-hearted legalism (see *Matt.* 23:23–24).

In our present age of self-indulgent licence, we cannot be reminded too often that our freedom in Christ (*Gal.* 5:1), is not a freedom to live as we please, but a freedom to live to please God. The gospel does not set us free from keeping God's commandments, but enables us, in the power of the Spirit, to keep them (see *Matt.* 5:17–20; *Rom.* 13:8–10). John is clearly concerned that his readers should well understand that Christian believers are to be *law-ful* and not *law-less*. This probably further reflects the influence that the false teachers were having in this and other churches.

4

Watch Yourselves

*F or many deceivers have gone out into the world, those who do not
confess the coming of Jesus Christ in the flesh. Such a one is the
deceiver and the antichrist. [8] Watch yourselves, so that you may not
lose what we have worked for, but may win a full reward. [9] Everyone
who goes on ahead and does not abide in the teaching of Christ, does
not have God. Whoever abides in the teaching has both the Father
and the Son* (2 John 7–9).

There is a striking connection between what John has just written and what now follows. In these verses John charges his
readers, 'Watch yourselves' (verse 8), because 'many deceivers
have gone out into the world' (verse 7). The word that introduces
verse 7, 'For', connects what John has just written with what he
now writes about the danger of false teaching. For John, protection
against 'the deceiver and the antichrist' is in large measure secured
by God's people loving one another and keeping God's commandments. Those who seek to 'deceive' them, and the arch-Deceiver
behind them, have open access into churches where there is both
an absence of mutual love and an absence of obedience to God's
commandments. The armour that repulses doctrinal error is not
only a mind saturated in God's truth, though that is vital, but also
a life that is filled with God's love and devoted to keeping his commandments.

In his First Letter, John wrote about 'false prophets' (4:2) who
had gone out into the world; now he describes them as 'deceivers
[who] have gone out into the world'. He is probably thinking of
people who once belonged to the church but who had abandoned
it (see *1 John* 2:19). They had 'gone out into the world' to pro-

claim their soul-destroying errors. John calls them 'deceivers' (see also *1 John* 2:26) and tells us that there were 'many' of them. Jesus had warned his disciples that 'False christs and false prophets will arise and perform signs and wonders, to lead astray, if possible, the elect' (*Mark* 13:22). He also exhorted them to 'Be on guard' (*Mark* 13:23).

At the heart of the deception of these false teachers was their denial that Jesus Christ had come in the flesh. This was a contradiction of the whole apostolic testimony concerning Jesus (see *John* 1:1, 14) and a denial of Jesus' witness to himself (see *John* 6:32–38; 8:58). It was nothing less than a denial of the incarnation. It is probable that these deceivers denied that God, who is Spirit (*John* 4:24), would ever identify himself with 'flesh'. And yet this is the glory and wonder of the gospel. God became what he was not, in order to redeem us from our sin and reconcile us to himself. If God's Son had not become flesh, we could never be saved. He became one with us in our humanity, so that 'from our side', as our representative Head (see *Rom.* 5:12–21), he might make atonement for sin.

The writer to the Hebrews affirms the truth and wonder of the incarnation: 'Since, therefore, the children share in flesh and blood, he himself likewise partook of the same things, that through death he might destroy the one who has the power of death, that is, the devil, and deliver all those who through fear of death were subject to life long slavery' (*Heb.* 2:14–15). Most doctrinal error springs from an unwillingness to bow before the clarity, however mysterious, of God's revelation in Christ. Unbelief is almost always due to a sinful refusal to acknowledge that God's ways are not our ways, that his thoughts are higher than our thoughts (see *Isa.* 55:8–9). To John everyone who denies the incarnation is 'the' deceiver and 'the' antichrist! Probably John means that they are the epitome and essence of error and wickedness. Nothing is more dishonouring to God and more destructive of the gospel than the heresies these deceivers taught. Once again we see how radically intolerant John, and indeed the whole Bible, is of false teaching. He lived in a multi-faith world, but he was absolutely sure that Jesus Christ is 'the way, the truth and the life' (*John* 14:6). It was John's commitment to the glory of Christ and his concern for the eternal good of sinners that caused him to write as he did. If the church today is embarrassed by John's language, it is only because it has, unlike John, little concern for Christ's glory and even less concern for the salvation of a world which even now 'lies in the power of the evil one' (*1 John* 5:19).

John proceeds to give two warnings to 'the elect lady and her children'.

First, in verse 8, he warns them, *'Watch yourselves, so that you may not lose what we have worked for, but may win a full reward.'* Personal and corporate watchfulness is a note that is sounded throughout the New Testament (see *Matt.* 26:41; *1 Pet.* 4:7; 5:8). What does it mean to 'watch oneself'? In the first place it surely means to recognize that none of us is invulnerable to Satan-inspired deception (see *1 Cor.* 10:12). Paul tells the Corinthians that 'we are not ignorant of his [Satan's] designs' (*2 Cor.* 2:11).

Satan is a designing deceiver. He has plans and stratagems that relentlessly seek our downfall (see *Eph.* 6:10–12). Personal watchfulness will also mean that we will pray – 'watch and pray'. In prayer we call upon the help of our gracious God to support and strengthen us in the good fight of the faith (*1 Tim.* 6:12). It will mean nothing less than putting on 'the whole armour of God, that (we) may be able to stand against the schemes of the devil' (*Eph.* 6:11). The reason why such watchfulness is absolutely necessary is 'so that you may not lose what we have worked for, but may win a full reward'.

John is clearly thinking here about the possibility of his friends losing, not their salvation, but the gracious reward that God gives to his faithful servants (see *1 Cor.* 3:8, 10–15; *Matt.* 20:1–16).

It is interesting to notice the connection between the 'you' and the 'we' in verse 8. John, with others, had worked hard to establish these believers in the truth of the gospel (compare also *1 Cor.* 3:9). Growth in grace takes place supremely in the context of the church (see *Eph.* 3:18; *1 Cor.* 12:1–26). It is hard to be precise about the significance of the 'full reward'. Perhaps John is thinking of *Matt.* 25:23, 'Well done, good and faithful servant.'

John's concern, however, is not only that they may not lose their 'full reward'. In verse 9 he warns them, 'Everyone who goes on ahead and does not abide in the teaching of Christ, does not have God.' The seriousness of denying God's revealed truth, particularly here that Jesus Christ has come in the flesh, is that those who do so do not 'have God', have no fellowship with him, do not in any sense belong to him. John does not specify precisely what he means by 'goes on ahead'. Most probably he is thinking of the false teachers who claimed superior 'knowledge', and that they had 'gone beyond' the apostolic teaching concerning Christ.

In his First Letter, John reminded his readers that they had been 'anointed by the Holy One' and possessed all knowledge. They knew the truth (*1 John* 2:21) and did not need to 'go on ahead' of 'the teaching of the Christ'. It is part of false teachers' deception that they claim to know more than everyone else. They refuse to 'abide in the teaching of Christ'. On the contrary, one of the marks of the children of God is that they 'listen' to Christ's voice (*John* 10:16) and are content to 'follow' him (*John* 10:27).

To 'abide in the teaching of Christ' simply means to believe that teaching, to be shaped by it, to be intellectually and affectionally content with it. It is the conviction of such people that God's Word is not only infallibly true; it is also completely sufficient (see *2 Tim.* 3:16–17). We do not need new revelations, because God has spoken his last and his best word in his Son, Jesus Christ (see *Heb.* 1:1–3).

John could hardly place more emphasis on the vital importance of right doctrine. God's revealed truth in Christ is not open to manipulation to suit the intellectual climate of the age. It is a body of truth 'once for all delivered to the saints' (*Jude* 3). To go on ahead, to claim superior enlightenment, is to leave God behind. God and his truth are inseparable. So, it is those who 'abide in the teaching' who possess 'both the Father and the Son'.

The absolute claims of the Christian gospel concerning Christ are offensive to the world. It would be content if the Christian faith was but one option among many. What it cannot tolerate is the gospel's teaching concerning Christ's uniqueness as God's eternal and only-begotten Son, the incarnate God, the only Mediator between God and man (*1 Tim.* 2:5).

5

Not Welcome

If anyone comes to you and does not bring this teaching, do not receive him into your house or give him any greeting, [11] for whoever greets him takes part in his wicked works (2 John 10–11).

So seriously does John take the threat of these false teachers and their deceptions that he commands his readers not to 'receive [them] into your house or give [them] any greeting'. These words need to be understood against the general biblical teaching that Christians are to 'seek to show hospitality' (*Rom.* 12:13) and to show practical kindness and mercy to enemies (see *Rom.* 12:20–21). Yet here John is uncompromising: 'If anyone [whoever they are, however respected and prominent they may be] comes to you and does not bring this teaching, do not receive him into your house or give him any greeting.' Christian hospitality does not extend to inviting soul-devouring, Christ-denying, wolves into our homes. Men and women who deny the fundamental truths of God's Word and who seek to spread their heresies are to be confronted, not welcomed.

If we are right in thinking that this Letter was addressed to a particular church, it would seem more likely that 'your house' refers to the congregation. John is then warning 'the elect lady and her children', God's household, against giving anyone who does not abide 'in the teaching of the Christ', that is, the apostolic gospel, the opportunity to spread their deceptions among God's people. However pleasant 'Christian' teachers are, 'If they do not speak according to this word' [God's revealed truth], it is because 'they have no light of dawn' (*Isa.* 8:20, NIV), and must be refused access to our churches.

Shepherds would have to be blind or stupid to allow wolves access to the sheepfold. John underlines the vital importance of guarding the flock of God, 'for whoever greets him [the false teacher] takes part in his wicked works'. A readiness to embrace religious teachers, notwithstanding their rejection of the gospel, involves us in their 'wicked works'. When the truth of God's revealed Word and the eternal good of lost sinners is at issue, Christ's church is to be uncompromising in its rejection of heresy. It is surely a deeply solemn thing when spiritual gullibility and naïve ecumenism make believers complicit in the 'wicked works' of false teachers.

Our Lord Jesus' prayer in *John* 17 has often been quietly neglected by evangelical Christians. We excuse our lack of visible unity by saying that our Christian unity is spiritual. That is true, but Jesus prayed that it would also be visible. However, it must never be forgotten that any visible Christian unity must be founded upon the apostolic gospel (see *John* 17:20). The unity for which our Lord Jesus prayed was a unity marked by truth, not a unity of ecclesiastical convenience. The intolerant language of John, and indeed of the Bible as a whole, sits uneasily with our multi-faith, post-modern world. But granted the New Testament's fundamental premise that 'in Christ God was reconciling the world to himself' (*2 Cor.* 5:19), John's language is not only understandable, it is necessary.

6

Final Greetings

T *hough I have much to write to you, I would rather not use paper and ink. Instead I hope to come to you and talk face to face, so that our joy may be complete.* *13* *The children of your elect sister greet you* (2 John 12–13).

John's brief conclusion is personal and affectionate. However helpful, and at times necessary, letters are, they cannot compare with a 'face-to-face' (literally *mouth-to-mouth*) encounter. The tone we speak in, the looks we convey, the gestures we instinctively use, all add colour, humanity and clarity to our bare words. Even God's eternal Word, his only-begotten Son, 'became flesh and dwelt among us' (*John* 1:14). So, John hopes to come to them soon, 'so that our joy may be complete' (see *1 John* 1:4).

John had heard the Lord Jesus speak about fullness of joy (see *John* 16:24), a joy that flows from an assured relationship with God in Christ, a joy that transcends all earthly circumstances (see *Phil.* 4:4). Here he anticipates the complete or full joy that is the fruit of Christians living in loving harmony with one another, as they are embraced together in the gospel of the Lord Jesus Christ.

His final word is a greeting from 'the children of your elect sister', that is, from the members of their sister church. The familial language highlights to the end the deep intimacy of Christian fellowship. God is our Father and we are his children. The church is the 'household of God' (*Eph.* 2:19; see also *Gal.* 6:10, 'the household of faith').

3 JOHN

*T*he elder to the beloved Gaius, whom I love in truth. [2] Beloved,
I pray that all may go well with you and that you may be in
good health, as it goes well with your soul. [3] For I rejoiced greatly
when the brothers came and testified to your truth, as indeed you are
walking in the truth. [4] I have no greater joy than to hear that my
children are walking in the truth. [5] Beloved, it is a faithful thing you
do in all your efforts for these brothers, strangers as they are, [6] who
testified to your love before the church. You will do well to send them
on their journey in a manner worthy of God. [7] For they have gone
out for the sake of the name, accepting nothing from the Gentiles.
[8] Therefore we ought to support people like these, that we may be fellow workers for the truth. [9] I have written something to the church,
but Diotrephes, who likes to put himself first, does not acknowledge
our authority. [10] So if I come, I will bring up what he is doing, talking
wicked nonsense against us. And not content with that, he refuses to
welcome the brothers, and also stops those who want to and puts them
out of the church. [11] Beloved, do not imitate evil but imitate good.
Whoever does good is from God; whoever does evil has not seen God.
[12] Demetrius has received a good testimony from everyone, and from
the truth itself. We also add our testimony, and you know that our
testimony is true. [13] I had much to write to you, but I would rather not
write with pen and ink. [14] I hope to see you soon, and we will talk face
to face. [15] Peace be to you. The friends greet you. Greet the friends,
every one of them (3 John).

L ike *1* and *2 John*, *3 John* has always been attributed by the
church to the apostle John. Indeed, 'The three Epistles and
the Gospel of John are so closely allied in diction, style, and general

outlook that the burden of proof lies with the person who would deny their common authorship.'[1]

John's Second and Third Letters show how important the Christian grace of hospitality was in the early church. In his Letter to the Romans, Paul urged his readers, 'Contribute to the needs of the saints and seek to show hospitality' (*Rom.* 12:13). The writer to the Hebrews similarly urged his readers, 'Do not neglect to do good and to share what you have, for such sacrifices are pleasing to God' (*Heb.* 13:16).

There was, however, the danger that unscrupulous men would take advantage of such generous hospitality and use it to serve their own ends and not those of God's people (this is the background to *2 John*). In *3 John* the concern is somewhat different. While Gaius was faithfully ministering to itinerant 'brothers', even though they were 'strangers' (verse 5), Diotrephes refused 'to welcome the brothers', and even wanted to stop others who were doing so and put them out of the church (verse 10).

3 John is yet another example of the statement in the *Westminster Confession of Faith* that 'the purest churches under heaven are subject both to mixture and error' (25.5). John is writing, not only to praise and encourage Gaius for his Christian grace, but also to correct an abuse that was dishonouring Christ and disfiguring the church's witness.

A unique feature of *3 John* is that, although John speaks of 'the name', clearly meaning the Lord Jesus Christ, he never actually uses the name 'Jesus Christ'.

---

[1] B. H. Streeter, *The Four Gospels*, revised edition (London: Macmillan, 1930), p. 460.

I

Greetings and Prayer

The elder to the beloved Gaius, whom I love in truth. ² Beloved, I pray that all may go well with you and that you may be in good health, as it goes well with your soul (3 John 1–2).

Unlike *2 John* which was written to a particular congregation, *3 John* was written to a particular individual, Gaius. John again describes himself as 'the elder' (see the comment on *2 John* 1). His Letter is addressed to 'the beloved Gaius'. Although there are several men of this name mentioned in the New Testament, there is nothing to indicate who exactly this Gaius was. It seems likely that he was a leader in a church to which John had already written regarding the support of itinerant Christian preachers (see verse 9). To John he was 'beloved'. Indeed, in the space of a few words, John three times expresses his love for this faithful, hospitable Christian. In particular, he describes him as one 'whom I love in truth'. As in *2 John* 1 there is no definite article before 'truth'. While it is possible grammatically that John is saying that his love for Gaius is rooted in 'the truth' of the gospel, and that they are together children of the truth, it is perhaps more likely that he is simply assuring Gaius that he loves him sincerely, genuinely. Christian love is to be 'genuine' (ἀνυπόκριτος, *Rom.* 12:9), without any trace of 'hypocrisy'.

Having identified to whom he is writing, John tells his 'beloved' friend that he is praying 'that all may go well with you, and that you may be in good health, as it goes well with your soul'. He is sure that it is going well with Gaius' soul, that his faith and love and service to the Lord 'goes well'. He is also concerned, however, that *everything* may go well with Gaius, body as well as soul. Our bodies matter. Our Lord Jesus Christ 'became flesh'; he fulfilled his saving mission in a 'body'. It is important that we never depreciate the body and somehow think it is a 'necessary evil'. It is our 'bodies' that we are to present to the Lord as living sacrifices (*Rom.* 12:1). 'Good health' enables us to serve the Lord with vigour.

2

Great Joy

For I rejoiced greatly when the brothers came and testified to your truth, as indeed you are walking in the truth. ⁴ I have no greater joy than to hear that my children are walking in the truth (3 John 3–4).

John proceeds to tell Gaius that he 'rejoiced when the brothers came and testified to your truth, as indeed you are walking in the truth'. Presumably these 'brothers' were itinerant evangelists, sent out, possibly from the church John served. These brothers had testified to Gaius' personal commitment to the truth. Nothing more rejoiced John's heart than hearing 'that my children are walking in the truth' (verse 4). God's truth, his revealed Word, is not simply a collection of truths to believe, it is a lifestyle to practise. We are to 'walk' in the truth, that is, we are to live out the truth in what we do and say and think. This is what Gaius was doing. There is a radical difference between merely confessing God's truth and having your life shaped and fashioned by his truth. Jesus spoke of religious leaders who honoured him with their lips, while their hearts were far from him (*Mark* 7:6). The test of true discipleship to Christ is that we walk in, or have our lives conformed to, God's truth. Indeed, Jesus said, 'Not everyone who says to me, "Lord, Lord", will enter the kingdom of heaven, but the one who does the will of my Father who is in heaven' (*Matt.* 7:21).

Once again we see how important and central 'the truth' was to Christ's apostles. It mattered profoundly to them what a person believed and how they lived. Paul similarly commanded Timothy to 'follow the pattern of sound words that you heard from me', and 'guard the good deposit entrusted to you' (*2 Tim.* 1:13–14). The truth is, essentially, what God has revealed concerning his Son, Jesus Christ. It is the apostolic testimony to the incarnation, life, death, resurrection, ascension and coming again of God's Son.

3

Welcoming Strangers

B *eloved, it is a faithful thing you do in all your efforts for these brothers, strangers as they are, ⁶ who testified to your love before the church. You will do well to send them on their journey in a manner worthy of God. ⁷ For they have gone out for the sake of the name, accepting nothing from the Gentiles. ⁸ Therefore we ought to support people like these, that we may be fellow workers for the truth* (3 John 5–8).

John again refers to Gaius as 'Beloved'. His language, and his actions, reflect Jesus' words in *John* 13:34–35. Above all things, Christians are to be known by the love they have for one another. John commends Gaius for his 'efforts' for the itinerating brothers. His kindness and care for them was 'a faithful thing'. Clearly Gaius' 'love' was demonstrated in practical kindness to these 'strangers'. They were 'brothers' even though they were 'strangers'. One of the identifying marks of Christian love is its willingness to reach beyond its own circle of family and friends (see *Matt.* 25:34–36; *Heb.* 13:2). God himself is the model of loving, not only strangers, but strangers who were his enemies (see *Rom.* 5:8, 10). When Paul exhorts the Christians in Rome 'to show hospitality', the word he uses means literally to 'love strangers' (*Rom.* 12;13).

These brothers, who were strangers to Gaius, 'testified to [his] love before the church'. John asks him, therefore, to 'send them on their journey in a manner worthy of God'. He does not specify what this will mean. Presumably, however, John is thinking of the kind generosity of God, 'who did not spare his own Son but gave him up for us all' (*Rom.* 8:32). Christian love is never to degenerate into mere sentimentality, but always be marked by practical, even self-denying, kindness (see *James* 2:14–17; *1 John* 3:16–18).

John highlights two further reasons why Gaius should support these brothers. First, 'For they have gone out for the sake of the name, accepting nothing from the Gentiles'. These brothers had left the security of family and friends 'for the sake of the name'. They were missionaries with no visible means of support. The gospel significance of their mission made them worthy to receive the support of God's people. The 'name', of course, is that of Jesus Christ (see *Acts* 4:12; 5:41). Christian missionaries, sent out in the name of Christ, have a claim upon the resources of God's people. These men accepted 'nothing from the Gentiles', that is from pagan unbelievers. They trusted the Lord to supply whatever they needed.

Second, when we support God's missionary servants we become 'fellow workers for the truth'. The work of the gospel involves all of God's people. As we support those whom God has set apart and the church has sent, with our hospitality, money and prayers, we share with them in their ministry. We are not all called to leave family and friends 'for the sake of the name', but we are all called to give ourselves and our God-given resources for Christ and his kingdom (see *Rom.* 12:1). This is a Christian imperative: it is what we 'ought' to do.

4

Satan's Sin

I have written something to the church, but Diotrephes, who likes to put himself first, does not acknowledge our authority. ¹⁰ So if I come, I will bring up what he is doing, talking wicked nonsense against us. And not content with that, he refuses to welcome the brothers, and also stops those who want to and puts them out of the church (3 John 9–10).

John now highlights a problem that was disfiguring the church and bringing great dishonour to God. He had earlier sent the church a letter (almost certainly not *1* or *2 John*), which a certain Diotrephes had ignored. He did not 'acknowledge our authority', presumably ignoring what John had written. John is possibly speaking of his own authority as an apostle of Christ (the 'royal we'), or of the authority of the leadership of the church he belongs to.

He tells us that Diotrephes 'likes to put himself first'. He was behaving with arrogant disregard towards church authority. Rather than acknowledge John's authority and welcome the missionary brothers, Diotrephes behaved arrogantly and refused to 'welcome the brothers'. At the root of his action was a desire for pre-eminence in the church, or possibly among the church's leaders. There was an absence in Diotrephes of the servant-spirit that so marked the life of the Lord Jesus Christ and that he commended to his disciples (see *Mark* 10:42–45).

The desire to put oneself first is the sin of the devil (see *Isa.* 14:12–23). It is a sin that puts a huge question mark over any Christian profession. In contrast to self-promotion, the Christian is urged to cultivate the mind of Christ 'who, though he was in the form of God, did not count equality with God a thing to be grasped, but made himself nothing, taking the form of a servant . . . [and] humbled himself by becoming obedient to the point of death, even the death on a cross' (*Phil.* 2:6–8).

Diotrephes' love of himself led him to deny authority, talk 'wicked nonsense' (we are not told what it was), refuse 'to welcome the brothers', stop those who wanted to welcome them, and ex-communicate them from the church. He was a man who brooked no rivals.

John informs Gaius, 'If I come, I will bring up what he is doing.' He is in effect saying that he will initiate public church discipline against Diotrephes. Too often arrogant men are allowed to thrive in Christ's church because no one has the courage to oppose them. Failure to exercise godly, necessary discipline has been the ruin of many churches.

5

Doing Good

*B*eloved, do not imitate evil but imitate good. Whoever does good
is from God; whoever does evil has not seen God. *¹² Demetrius
has received a good testimony from everyone, and from the truth
itself. We also add our testimony, and you know that our testimony
is true* (3 John 11–12).

John's counsel to Gaius not to 'imitate evil but [to] imitate good'
must be seen in the light of what he has just written about
Diotrephes, who was a model of evil. Gaius must not make
arrogant Diotrephes a model to follow. Arrogant men can exude
an aura of appeal, but their behaviour is 'evil'. Everyone who 'likes
to be first' is buying in to the mindset and lifestyle of 'the evil
one'. On the contrary, Gaius is to 'imitate good'. Christ himself is
the essence of all goodness. 'He went about doing good' (*Acts*
10:38).

For John, the practice of doing good, of not behaving with arrogant self-importance but acting with servant-like humility towards
others, reveals that we are 'from God', the God who 'so loved the
world that he gave his only Son' (*John* 3:16). On the contrary,
'whoever does evil has not seen God'. In his First Letter, John has
told us, 'No one has ever seen God' (*1 John* 4:12). Here the impli-
cation is that if we do good we have 'seen God'. It is true that God
'is the blessed and only Sovereign, the King of kings and Lord of
lords, who alone has immortality, who dwells in unapproachable
light, whom no one has ever seen or can see' (*1 Tim.* 6:15–16). It
is, no less true, however, that with the eye of faith believers behold
God and his glory (*2 Cor.* 3:18). To 'see God', in John's thinking,
is almost synonymous with being 'born of God'. Those who have
been born of God do good and do not sin (see *1 John* 3:9).

Once again John has affirmed that moral conformity to God's commandments marks us out as his children (see *1 John* 2:3–6).

John mentions now a certain 'Demetrius' (verse 12). One other Demetrius is mentioned in the New Testament (see *Acts* 19:23, 38). Whoever this man was, John wants Gaius to know that he is a Christian with godly credentials. Possibly he is one of the missionary strangers, perhaps even their leader. He had 'received a good testimony from everyone'. Everyone who knew, or had known, Demetrius spoke well of him. He was also commended by 'the truth itself'. John probably means that the truth he confessed and the life he lived were all of a piece. He did not confess Christ with his lips but deny him with his behaviour (see *Mark* 7:6–7). Thirdly, John and his fellow church leaders warmly commended him, 'and you know that our testimony is true'.

John never tires of reminding us that true faith in the Lord Jesus Christ is always supported by a godly lifestyle (see *Heb.*12:14; *Matt.* 5:8). He also again sounds the note that the Christian life is lived in fellowship with God's church. Believers are members of Christ's body. They are called to live in brotherly fellowship, learning together 'what is the breadth and length and height and depth, and to know the love of Christ that surpasses knowledge' (*Eph.* 3:18–19).

6

Final Greetings

I had much to write to you, but I would rather not write with pen and ink. ¹⁴ I hope to see you soon, and we will talk face to face. ¹⁵ Peace be to you. The friends greet you. Greet the friends, every one of them (3 John 13–15).

John's conclusion and greeting is similar to *2 John* 12-13. He is hopeful of visiting Gaius soon. He has 'much to write', but he would rather communicate with his friend 'face to face'. In our increasingly impersonal, cyberspace age, Christians need to make face-to-face communication a priority. We are not disembodied beings. Meaningful friendship and fellowship requires personal contact. Smiles and sighs convey a wealth of meaning that the written word cannot express: 'And the Word became flesh . . . and we have seen his glory' (*John* 1:14).

'Peace be to you' was a common Hebrew greeting. 'Peace' meant more than 'have a quiet, untroubled life'; though Gaius would perhaps have settled for that in the circumstances. It means to make whole and bring to perfection (see also the comment on *2 John* 3). For Christians, it would be difficult not to think of Jesus' greeting to his disciples on the evening of his resurrection, 'Peace be with you' (*John* 20:21), expressing the transforming bounty of God's goodness to his people.

The concluding words are significant: 'The friends greet you. Greet the friends, every one of them.' Everyone mattered. No one was to be omitted from the apostle's greeting. Every Christian is to recognize every other Christian as a 'friend'. We are friends because Christ has made us his friends (see *John* 15:14–15).

Group Study Guide

SCHEME FOR GROUP BIBLE STUDY
(Covers 13 Weeks; before each study read the passage indicated and the chapters from this book shown below.)

STUDY PASSAGE	CHAPTERS
1. *1 John* 1:1–10	Introduction and 1–2
2. *1 John* 2:1–6	3–4
3. *1 John* 2:7–14	5–6
4. *1 John* 2:15–17	7
5. *1 John* 2:18–27	8
6. *1 John* 2:28–3:10	9–11
7. *1 John* 3:11–24	12–14
8. *1 John* 4:1–6	15
9. *1 John* 4:7–21	16–17
10. *1 John* 5:1–12	18–19
11. *1 John* 5:13–21	20
12. *2 John*	*2 John* section, 1–6
13. *3 John*	*3 John* section, 1–6

This Study Guide has been prepared for group Bible study, but it can also be used individually. Those who use it on their own may find it helpful to keep a note of their responses in a notebook.

The way in which group Bible studies are led can greatly enhance their value. A well-conducted study will appear as though it has been easy to lead, but that is usually because the leader has worked hard and planned well. Clear aims are essential.

LET'S STUDY THE LETTERS OF JOHN

AIMS

In all Bible study, individual or corporate, we have several aims:

1. To gain an understanding of the original meaning of the particular passage of Scripture;

2. To apply this to ourselves and our own situation;

3. To develop some specific ways of putting the biblical teaching into practice.

2 Timothy 3:16–17 provides a helpful structure. Paul says that Scripture is useful for:

    (i)   teaching us;

    (ii)   rebuking us;

    (iii)   correcting, or changing us;

    (iv)   training us in righteousness.

Consequently, in studying any passage of Scripture, we should always have in mind these questions:

What does this passage teach us (about God, ourselves, etc.)?

Does it rebuke us in some way?

How can its teaching transform us?

What equipment does it give us for serving Christ?

In fact, these four questions alone would provide a safe guide in any Bible study.

PRINCIPLES

In group Bible study we meet in order to learn about God's Word and ways 'with all the saints' (*Eph.* 3:18). But our own experience, as well as Scripture, tells us that the saints are not always what they *are* called to be in every situation – including group Bible study! Leaders ordinarily have to work hard and prepare well if the work of the group is to be spiritually profitable. The following guidelines for leaders may help to make this a reality.

Preparation:

1. Study and understand the passage yourself. The better prepared and more sure of the direction of the study you are, the more likely it is that the group will have a beneficial and enjoyable study. Ask: What are the main things this passage is saying? How can this be made clear? This is not the same question as the more common 'What does this passage "say to you"?', which expects a reaction rather than an exposition of the passage. Be clear about that distinction yourself, and work at making it clear in the group study.

2. On the basis of your own study form a clear idea *before* the group meets of (i) the main theme(s) of the passage which should be opened out for discussion, and (ii) some general conclusions the group ought to reach as a result of the study. Here the questions which arise from 2 Timothy 3:16–17 should act as our guide.

3. The guidelines and questions which follow may help to provide a general framework for each discussion; leaders should use them as starting places which can be further developed. It is usually helpful to have a specific goal or theme in mind for group discussion, and one is suggested for each study. But even more important than tracing a single theme is understanding the teaching and the implications of the passage.

Leading the Group:

1. Announce the passage and theme for the study, and begin with prayer. In group studies it may be helpful to invite a different person to lead in prayer each time you meet.

2. Introduce the passage and theme, briefly reminding people of its outline and highlighting the content of each subsidiary section.

3. Lead the group through the discussion questions. Use your own if you are comfortable in doing so; those provided may be used, developing them with your own points. As discussion proceeds, continue to encourage the group first of all to discuss the significance of the passage (teaching) and only then its application (meaning for us). It may be helpful to write important points and applications on a board by way of summary as well as visual aid.

[121]

4. At the end of each meeting, remind members of the group of their assignments for the next meeting, and encourage them to come prepared. Be sufficiently prepared as the leader to give specific assignments to individuals, or even couples, or groups, to come with specific contributions.

5. Remember that you are the leader of the group! Encourage clear contributions, and do not be embarrassed to ask someone to explain what they have said more fully or to help them to do so ('Do you mean . . . ?').

Most groups include the 'over-talkative', the 'over-silent' and the 'red-herring raisers'! Leaders must control the first, encourage the second and redirect the third! Each leader will develop his or her own most natural way of doing that; but it will be helpful to think out what that is before the occasion arises! The first two groups can be helped by some judicious direction of questions to specific individuals or even groups (for example, 'Jane, you know something about this from personal experience . . .'); the third by redirecting the discussion to the passage itself ('That is an interesting point, but isn't it true that this passage really concentrates on . . . ?'). It may be helpful to break the group up into smaller groups sometimes, giving each subgroup specific points to discuss and to report back on. A wise arranging of these smaller groups may also help each member to participate.

More important than any techniques we may develop is the help of the Spirit enabling us to understand and to apply the Scriptures. Have and encourage a humble, prayerful spirit.

6. Keep faith with the schedule; it is better that some of the group wished the study could have been longer than that others are inconvenienced by it stretching beyond the time limits set.

7. Close in prayer. As time permits, spend the closing minutes in corporate prayer, encouraging the group to apply what they have learned in praise and thanks, intercession and petition.

STUDY 1

Introduction and Chapters 1–2

AIM: To study the context of John's Letter and appreciate the communion we have with God.

1. Why did John write this Letter?

2. Why is Jesus described as 'the life'?

3. 'The Christian's fellowship is with the Triune God.' What does this mean? How will this fellowship or communion express itself in personal and public worship?

4. 'God is light.' What does this mean? How should this truth impact the Christian life?

5. What does it mean to 'walk in the light'?

6. How is God able 'to forgive our sins and to cleanse us from all unrighteousness'?

STUDY 2

Chapters 3–4

AIM: To grasp the richness of salvation in Christ and the relationship between gospel and law.

1. What does it mean for Jesus to be our 'advocate with the Father'?

2. In what sense is Jesus the propitiation 'for the sins of the whole world'?

3. How should a Christian keep God's commandments?

4. Why does a failure to keep God's commandments reveal that the truth is not in us?

5. In what sense is God's love perfected when we keep his Word?

STUDY 3

Chapters 5–6

AIM: To study John's teaching on abiding in the light and what that means for our relationships.

1.   How can the 'old commandment' be 'at the same time' a new commandment?

2.   What is 'the darkness' that is passing away?

3.   Who are the brothers we are to love? What challenges does this bring to our understanding of the Christian life?

4.   In what ways do we grow in our knowledge of God?

5.   Why is it important that God's Word abides in us? Should Christians take more seriously the reality and activity of 'the evil one'? (read *Eph.* 6:10–13)

STUDY 4

Chapter 7

AIM: To understand why Christians should not love the world.

1.   What does loving the world mean?

2.   In what ways do you think people today are drawn to loving the world?

3.   What will help Christians not to love the world?

4.   We read in *John* 3:16, 'For God so loved the world . . .' What is the difference between God's love for the world and the love for the world that John condemns?

5.   In what sense is 'the world passing away'? How, in the light of this, can Christians live distinctively different lives?

STUDY 5

Chapter 8

AIM: To be alert to the danger of being deceived by false teaching.

1.   Who were the 'antichrists' and what were they seeking to do?

2.   'The church has always been a mixed multitude.' Why should this be so? How should this fact shape the leadership and preaching ministry of a church?

3.   What were the particular heresies of the antichrists? Can you recognize these errors in the church today?

4.   How can we guard against being deceived by false teaching (see *1 John* 2:24)?

5.   'You have no need that anyone should teach you.' What does John mean?

STUDY 6

Chapters 9–11

AIM: To deepen our understanding of what it means to be a child of God.

1.   What other passages in the New Testament speak of Christ's personal return? How are Christians to live in the light of the Second Coming?

2.   What is the connection between the new birth and practising righteousness (see *1 John* 2:29)?

3.   How do rebel sinners become children of God (see *John* 1:12)? What are the 'birthmarks' that distinguish God's children?

4.   What does John mean when he writes, 'sin is lawlessness'?

5.   How and when did Christ 'destroy the works of the devil' (*1 John* 3:8)?

STUDY 7

Chapters 12–14

AIM: To understand the obligation Christians have to love one another and to appreciate the seriousness of not loving fellow believers.

1.   Why should Christians love one another?

2.   What does it mean to be 'like Cain'?

3.   How do we begin to understand what love is (see *1 John* 3:16–18)?

4.   How can we express our love in 'deed and in truth'? (Read *Matt.* 25:34–40)

5.   What does it mean, 'God is greater than our heart'? How does this truth comfort the believer?

STUDY 8

Chapter 15

AIM: To learn how to 'test the spirits' and appreciate the importance of doctrine.

1.   How do we 'test the spirits'?

2.   What truths does 'the spirit of the antichrist' deny? Why?

3.   How have God's children overcome the false prophets? In what sense does God's indwelling presence enable us to overcome false teaching?

4.   'They are from the world.' What kind of thinking and behaviour would show that someone was 'from the world'?

5.   How can we distinguish between 'the Spirit of truth' and 'the spirit of error'?

STUDY 9

Chapters 16–17

AIM: To study in more detail God's love and why love should be the distinguishing mark of a Christian.

1.   Why should Christians love one another? 'Likeness is the proof of relationship.' Discuss.

2.   What did it mean for Jesus Christ 'to be the propitiation for our sins'?

3.   What is the connection between, 'No one has ever seen God' and 'if we love one another, God abides in us and his love is perfected in us' (*1 John* 4:12)?

4.   What does it mean to confess 'that Jesus is the Son of God' (*1 John* 4:15)?

5.   How is 'love perfected with us' (*1 John* 4:17)?

6.   How does 'perfect love [cast] out fear' (*1 John* 4:18)?

STUDY 10

Chapters 18–19

AIM: To study further the relationship between loving God and keeping his commandments and appreciate the certainty of God's testimony concerning his Son.

1.   What is the significance of 'everyone who loves the Father loves whoever has been born of him' for ecumenical relationships?

2.   In what sense are God's commands wings that help us fly, not weights that hold us down?

3.   How does 'faith' enable us to 'overcome the world'?

4.   Why does John write of Jesus as 'he who came by water and blood'?

5.   How did or does the Spirit testify to who Jesus is?

6.   How would you know that you had 'life'?

STUDY 11

Chapter 20

AIM: To deepen our understanding of the great salvation Christians have in Jesus Christ.

1. How may we know that we have eternal life?

2. '[If] we ask anything according to his will he hears us.' How should this truth shape our prayers?

3. 'I am my brother's keeper.' How are Christians to pastor one another in the fellowship of the church?

4. Why is the evil one unable to touch the child of God (*1 John* 5:18)?

5. What 'idols' most endanger Christians in your part of the world today?

STUDY 12

2 John Section, Chapters 1–6

AIM: To cultivate deeper self-watchfulness, so that we may not lose our reward (*2 John* 8).

1. What does it mean for God's truth to abide in us?

2. 'Christian love is more a command to obey than a sentiment to cultivate.' Discuss.

3. How can we better cultivate a spirit of self-watchfulness?

4. Why should we not welcome heretical teachers into our homes?

STUDY 13

3 John Section, Chapters 1–6

AIM: To understand better the importance of Christian hospitality and the support of Christian workers.

1.   What can we learn from John's prayer in *3 John* 2? Consider also Paul's prayers in *Eph.* 1 and 3, and *Col.* 1.

2.   Welcoming 'strangers' can be problematic in our age.
What safeguards can help us not to be gullible?

3.   The sin of Diotrephes is only too common in the church.
What help has the Lord given us to protect us from falling into this
great evil?

4.   Why is church discipline apparently rarely exercised in
churches today?

5.   'Any friend of Jesus is a friend of mine.' How can we
guard against becoming sectarian in our Christian faith (see *Mark*
9:38–41)?

FOR FURTHER READING

The following books are recommended for study of the Letters of John:

JOHN STOTT, *The Epistles of John* (Tyndale Press, London, 1964; revised edition, 1988).

DAVID JACKMAN, *The Message of John's Letters* (Inter-Varsity Press, Leicester, England; Downers Grove, Illinois, USA, 1988).

ROBERT CANDLISH, *A Commentary on 1 John* (1866, 1877; reprinted, Banner of Truth, Edinburgh, 1993).

ROBERT LAW, *The Tests of Life* (1909; reprinted, Baker Book House, Grand Rapids, 1982).